The Courage To Be Yourself

The Courage
To Be Yourself

A Woman's Guide
to Growing
Beyond Emotional
Dependence

Sue Patton Thoele

Conari Press
Berkeley, CA

ISBN: 0-943233-25-9

Thoele, Sue Patton.
    The courage to be yourself : a woman's guide to growing
beyond emotional dependence / Sue Patton Thoele.
        p.   cm.
    Includes bibiliogrphical references (p.   )
    ISBN 0-943233-25-9 : $10.95
    1. Women—Psychology. 2. Dependency (Psychology) 3. Self-
help techniques.   I. Title.
HQ1206.T465   1991
158'.1'082—dc20

                                        91-26657
                                        CIP

Dedication

*In loving memory of
my courageous mother,
Virginia Faris Patton,
who had a special talent
for listening.*

Acknowledgments

I want to thank my dear friend, Bonnie Hampton, for walking the first miles of this book with me and steadfastly believing I could "go it alone." Also a big thank-you to Joyce McKay, Polly Ostrofe, and Irene Frazier for their insightful expertise and valuable time. I'm so grateful for my publishers, Julie Bennett and Mary Jane Ryan, who guide me with wisdom and determination and gently edit my work. For the inspiration they have given me, I want to thank each of the writers whose words I've quoted here. Extra special thanks to my husband and partner, Gene Thoele, for all his love, support, and enthusiasm. He provides much-needed hugs when I am battered by computer-frustration fatigue, and he is fun to live with, besides!

The Courage To Be Yourself

Part Two
Facing the Dragons in the Dungeon

Part Three
Healing: Owning Your Own Excellence

Foreword

The root of the word "courage" is the Latin word *cor*, meaning "the heart." In this book, Sue Patton Thoele en-cour-ages or gives heart to the reader on the difficult and challenging steps through fear and emotional dependence. She guides women through the dis-cour-agement of self, others, and society, towards increased self-esteem and personal empowerment.

As a self-esteem specialist, I value this book because people who are emotionally dependent tend to have low self-esteem. They try to gain a sense of worth through what they do, how they perform, how they look, who they are with, what they have. They hope that others will notice and approve of them; only then will they be okay. As people pleasers and approval seekers, they are out of control of their *self-esteem.*

As we grow in emotional independence, we become more pleasing to ourselves. Instead of needing to impress, please or prove to others that we are okay, we affirm it for ourselves—and self-esteem increases.

Everyone is looking for models. In *The Courage to Be Yourself,* the author nudges, inspires, and supports women in filling in their developmental holes so they can become developmentally whole. In sharing her struggles, triumphs, and wisdom, Sue Thoele illuminates and models the path of courage for others.

Dr. Louise Hart,
author of *The Winning Family:*
Increasing Self-Esteem in Your Children and Yourself

Part One

Finding The
Courage
To Be Yourself

Introduction

*T*he *Courage to Be Yourself* evolved out of small groups and seminars, led by myself and my dear friend, Bonnie Hampton. In them we work on the common fears and emotional dependencies of women. Our goal is to provide simple but powerful tools for helping women grow beyond emotional dependence. In our groups and seminars we share techniques and insights that help many women in our private psychotherapy practices and also help us on our ever-evolving personal journeys toward having the courage to be ourselves.

One of my main goals orignally in writing this book was to help women love and appreciate themselves—to see how wonderful we are—because so often we feel an obligation to undervalue ourselves. I have been gratified by the letters I've received from readers who said that reading *The Courage to Be Yourself* made them love and accept themselves more rather than less and gave them the encouragement to "keep on keeping on" even when the going got tough. In the four years since the book first came out, I have learned so much from my readers that I wanted to incorporate both what I learned on my life's path as well as what I have discovered from the women I have been privilege to hear from.

Every one of the true stories and examples related in this book describes an important stage in a woman's experience of learning to be herself. The stories prove that we women can have the courage to be uniquely ourselves—that emotional independence is, in fact, our birthright, our privilege, and our responsibility.

CHAPTER 1

Courage:
You Can Have It!

*I have met brave women who are
exploring the outer edge of
human possibility, with no history to
guide them, and with a courage to
make themselves vulnerable that I find
moving beyond words.*

-Gloria Steinem

*A*re you often filling the wants and needs of others without having your own met? Do deadlines and difficult people leave you feeling frazzled? Do you feel overworked and under-appreciated? Do you grapple with self-limiting fears? Are you more an enemy than a friend to yourself?

Despite the tremendous changes of the last thirty years, many women will still answer "yes" to the above questions. Often we are caught in a tangled web of emotional dependence, afraid to express who we really are.

What Is Emotional Dependence?

Emotional dependence means needing to have others to survive, wanting others to "do it for us," and depending on others to give us our self-image, make our decisions, and take care of us financially. When we are emotionally dependent, we look to others for our happiness, our "self"-concept, and our emotional well-being. We give up what we want and need out of fear of rejection, abandonment, or confrontation.

Being emotionally dependent puts us at the mercy of our fears and other people's whims and severely limits our freedom to be ourselves. When we are emotionally dependent, we believe that others hold the key to our well-being, that

5

they must know better than we do what is good for us. Or we believe that, in order to gain and hold someone's love, we must give ourselves away.

Before I ever heard the term *emotional dependence* I knew that, in some mysterious way, I turned my life over to other people. It didn't really matter who they were—my parents, husband, kids, friends, co-workers. If they were happy with me, then I could be happy. If they approved of me, then I felt worthwhile. If they granted permission, then I believed it was okay for me to do or be something. I looked to others to give me the Good Housekeeping Seal of Approval before I was confident enough to take a step or a stand. I wasn't myself; I was whomever I thought the person I was trying to please wanted me to be. Since I wasn't a mind reader, no matter what form I pretzeled myself into, I wasn't able to please everyone all of the time. But I tried. That's emotional dependence!

Denying or sacrificing ourselves on the alter of others' expectations—or what we perceive to be their expectations— leaves us with no *self*. Without an awareness of our self, the courage to express who we are, and the willingness to experience the discomfort and exhilaration that follows, we are not truly living. We are existing merely as mirrors, reflecting other people's lives. Until we are able to be our unique and beautiful (and, sometimes, ugly and mundane) selves, we cannot truly love either ourselves or others, and love is what life is all about.

Why do so many women have problems with emotional dependence? As many researchers have shown, notably Carol Gilligan in *In a Different Voice*, women have a deep need for emotional connectedness and intimacy. That's not all bad. In fact, that desire is what makes us such wonderful lovers, friends, and mothers. But when that need is not balanced with the need be our own person, we can become emotionally dependent, losing sight of ourselves and all our capabilities.

We become afraid of anything that seems to threaten our connections to others. Being *dis*connected can feel life threatening and is, therefore, terrifying to us. Out of our terror we often do exactly what we are afraid others will do—we abandon ourselves, littering the sides of our personal life-road with forsaken desires, goals, and talents.

Fear—of not being loved, of abandonment, of being thought to be selfish—is the main thing that keeps us bound in the chains of emotional dependence. Therefore, our two most difficult challenges are to truly believe it is okay for us to be ourselves and to learn to live with, move through, and heal our fears.

Until several years ago, I was run by my fears. For example, I was deeply afraid of rejection or of offending anyone and would go to great lengths to avoid disagreement of any kind. But very few people who knew me would have said, "Wow, there's a woman who is really afraid!" I hid it well. And so, I was to learn, did countless other women.

Unfortunately, many of us have allowed fear to block our awareness of our inborn strengths. I myself used to be a master at doing that. Although other people perceived me as an independent person, I frequently felt I was only playing at being grown-up. Others saw me as successful and mature, but I wasn't fooling myself; inside, I felt buffeted by other people's moods, a helpless leaf in any storm. I knew that I hadn't taken responsibility for my own life, and I was afraid to do so.

Even though I had a master's degree in counseling and had been in private practice for several years, inwardly I felt I was "just a wife and mother." Sure, I had performed the work of an adult person, leading groups and seeing clients, but inside, I felt like a little girl dressing up and playing at these roles, hoping to gain the approval of others.

What changed? A great deal! I turned forty, met a wonder-

7

ful woman friend who wouldn't let me lie to myself, and, most important, I began to really listen to myself. Each of us has a "still, small voice" inside that speaks to us continuously. The trouble is, we seldom listen. Yet, if we let it, our inner authentic self can guide us unerringly. You, too, can hear the voice inside you that will help you to have the courage to become who you really are.

Courage: An Everyday Actuality

What exactly is courage? Courage is the ability to do what needs to be done, or feel what needs to be felt, in spite of fear. It's the willingness to risk or act even when we are frightened or in pain.

If you want to be emotionally independent and have more courage, you can. In fact, you already have a great deal of courage. We seldom think much about the courage we exert in simple, "normal" situations: having a baby, going to work day after day, sustaining relationships. It takes courage to fall in love, be honest with ourselves, survive a loss, move away from home, share a fear with a friend, ask for a raise, get a divorce, take on a job that challenges us, or tell someone when we're angry or hurt. Try writing down a list of things you've done even though you felt afraid. Those were acts of courage. Sometimes just getting up in the morning and proceeding with your life takes tremendous courage!

So, as I hope you can see now, you already have courage. Being courageous, and moving toward a fuller realization of our own authentic self, is a natural process. What is it that keeps us from realizing our full, courageous potential? *Fear!* What do we fear? We fear the unknown, anything that has been painful for us in the past, or anything that feels different and risky.

Actually risk has an entirely different side, too. With the right attitude, we can experience risk as exhilarating and creative. Risk is necessary for change, and change is necessary for growth. Growth is inevitable. We *will* grow, but will it be toward freedom or toward fearfulness? In order to be free we need to learn to honor our fears but not allow them to control our lives.

Bringing our fears out into the open and talking honestly about them helps us work through them. An unspoken fear is much more powerful than one that is shared.

The trouble is, we're afraid to talk about our fears because we think others will see us as too emotional, immature, or foolish. So we keep quiet, thus creating a self-enclosed inner world in which we condemn ourselves for feeling as we do and believe we're the only fearful people we know. Our fear creates crippling isolation. But as we risk voicing our fear and find it accepted gently by others, it loses its power.

The Co-Dependent Cage

For the first time in marriage, I have an equal say in our lives. I don't know why I allowed myself ever to do otherwise. I finally grew up and decided that I didn't need guidance or leadership from a father; what I needed was a friend, and that's what I have in Robert—a loving best friend.
-Mary Tyler Moore

In the almost four years since *The Courage to Be Yourself* was first published much has been written and taught about emotional dependence using the name *co-dependence*. The term *co-dependent* is often linked to being in a relationship with someone who is dependent on drugs or alcohol, but it is far more pervasive than that. We can be co-dependent with our husbands, kids, co-workers—even our dog or parakeet.

Being co-dependent means we consistently put others' needs, wants, and demands before our own--in other words, emotional dependence. Instead of gaining our self-esteem, self-motivation, and self-worth from ourselves, we rely on others to provide those feelings for us. When we turn our lives over to someone or something else, we are in a co-dependent cage. In that cage we become drugged by denial and depression!

If you feel that you have even a toe caught in the "co-cage," muster up your courage and find a friend or group of people who can help you spring free. Serving a life sentence as a co-dependent is tantamount to an emotional death penalty. Breaking out of the co-dependence cage is a life-giving escape. I have every confidence that you can do it. If I, who spent many years peering through the bars of co-dependence yearning for the freedom of emotional autonomy and independence, can do it, so can you.

Finding The Way To Ourselves

We all know now that women have a tendency, in greater or lesser degrees, to be emotionally dependent in their relationships. But how do we free ourselves from the trap?

I love the Irish proverb that says: You've got to do your own growing, no matter how tall your grandfather was. It's true. We will do our own growing eventually, so why let fear seduce us into inaction? An excellent way to overcome the paralysis that often accompanies fear is to join a group of women who are working on issues similar to our own. There are co-dependency seminars, Al-Anon, and other support groups everywhere. They can be found by calling your local mental health department, Alcoholics Anonymous, or by asking friends.

The most important thing the women in our seminars do is learn to talk openly about how they feel. As we share our shortcomings, secrets, fears, hostilities, joys, and disappointments, we realize we are not alone. Breaking out of isolation gives us permission to fully experience our feelings and then work through them.

Katy, a sweet, soft-spoken woman, sheepishly told me I couldn't possibly guess what she had discovered in one of our seminars. She was certain I'd be shocked and horrified to know that the main stress in her life related to her husband. Of course, I was neither shocked nor surprised. I know her husband, and he's a good man; but I also know that many women who are in relationships with good men feel stressed by their partners. In Katy's case, the mere reassurance from another woman that she wasn't alone in her unrevealed feelings, and that she wasn't a terrible person for having them, gave her the freedom to accept what she was really feeling.

Knowing and accepting our true feelings is an essential step in moving beyond emotional dependence toward the ability to be ourselves. It takes an enormous amount of courage to be emotionally independent because we have been taught to believe that our natural role is as an adjunct to other people—a helpmate, not an equal. However, the concept of inequality is obsolete. Having the courage to be who we really are is our natural birthright. If this is the case, then why is it so difficult for many of us to be ourselves, enjoy emotional independence, and have satisfying, equal relationships?

Establishing new patterns of beliefs and behaviors is always hard. We naturally seem to gravitate to the familiar even when it is uncomfortable. Giving ourselves permission to move into the uncharted waters of emotional independence and create new patterns for our lives takes courage and commitment.

Though it's often hard for us to give up the old habit of asking, "Mother, may I?" (or Father, or Husband), we're living in an age when we have unprecedented opportunities to make our own decisions—to be ourselves. As we unravel our emotional dependencies, we learn that no one can fill us with confidence, independence, and a sense of inner worth but ourselves, with the help of whatever we interpret as our Higher Source.

Another very important piece of the courage-to-be-your-self puzzle is the awareness that the most essential and important connection we can make is with ourselves! We have heard this so often lately that we know it in our heads, but it is difficult to really believe it in our hearts, because we have been socialized to conclude that our commitment is to others and our job is self sacrifice. A pervasive underlying belief women grow up carrying is that they come last, if at all. Yet, without a deep commitment to ourselves, we cannot truly relate healthily to others.

Yearning to have my inner dependent and insecure feelings match my outer independent and successful demeanor, I began to search for ways to free myself from the tyranny of fear and learn how to express who I really was. It has been a great adventure—sometimes terrifying, often exciting, but always educational. Since I began my quest to find Sue, I have felt alive.

Being emotionally independent doesn't mean that we're selfish and self-centered or unavailable to others. It does mean that we're centered in an awareness of who we are—no longer fragmented by fear or unrealistic demands from ourselves or others. An emotionally independent woman is a happier, more loving and giving woman. As we find the freedom to express who we really, uniquely are, we create a climate around ourselves in which others can also grow and be healed. Freed from the torment of looking outside ourselves for approval, and empowered by having our own identity, we have more to give. Plus, our lives are enhanced by a spirit of lightness and spontaneity.

The Courage to Be Yourself is brimming with practical, proven methods to assist you in your quest to live authentically and happily by expressing who you truly are. By using the concepts and examples in these pages you will become aware of your fears and learn how to overcome them. Freed from the shackles of fear, you can then give yourself permission to own your own excellence and live up to your highest potential. Although *The Courage to Be Yourself* contains no pat answers, it is filled with ideas and exercises designed to help you move from emotional dependence to emotional independence.

Even as we make progress, we may long to return to the easy fantasy that it's okay to be emotionally dependent, that our men will take care of us, that it's their responsibility to keep us safe and support us. To *really know* that the buck stops with ourselves is frightening; but it's also extremely freeing to realize that we can be independent, confident, and in control of ourselves. We are all—men and women—called to grow up, to assume responsibility for ourselves. As grown-ups we are better able to love, independently, interdependently, and joyfully.

We women are wonderfully courageous: we have what it takes to overcome our fear-full inner dragons and live our lives expressing our true selves. I have been honored to walk with many women as they courageously tamed their dragons and surmounted obstacles and traumas that had once nearly destroyed their faith in themselves. Usually we teach what we need to learn the most, and that is certainly true in my case.

So, as you read these pages, know that we are walking together. Live gently with yourself as you continue your journey toward being who you authentically are. Be patient with yourself, and don't try to go it alone.

CHAPTER 2

Facets
Of Emotional
Dependence

*A woman's public identity is her
husband's and her
private identity, her children's.*

-Virginia Woolf

*E*motional dependence is many faceted and can rear its depressive head in a host of different ways. Anytime we come away from an encounter with someone feeling used or abused—not having stood up for ourselves or what we believed—it's a pretty sure bet we have acted, or not acted, out of an emotionally dependent internal space. When we find ourselves believing it's not okay for us to have a self who can come first—at least part of the time—when we know that our "self"-concept is really an "other"-concept, or when we suppress our feelings in order to please someone else, we have undoubtedly come face to face with a facet of our own emotional dependence. A good question to ask ourselves at a time such as this is: What was I afraid of that made me act this way?

"I Have Rights! Okay?"

Women are waking up to the realization that they do have emotional and practical rights, that it is okay, and even healthy, for us to take care of ourselves and honor our own needs. We're beginning, tentatively and sometimes militantly, to act on these realizations. I have a cartoon that depicts the difficulty of the process: A woman is sitting at a restaurant table with a man. She says, "I have independence!

17

I ask for what I need. I am taking responsibility for my life." In the final frame, she reaches across the table and grabs the man by the arms and asks anxiously, "Is that okay with you?"

Throughout history, women have been considered men's helpmates, secretaries, and moral supporters. *Behind* every successful man, as the saying goes, stands a good woman. Fortunately, we're living in an age in which that outdated saying is changing to: Side by side stand successful men and women.

Although we may accept and believe in our equality with deep conviction, we often need to work hard on our ability to honor our limits and boundaries, to stand up for our rights and really feel that we can expect treatment such as kindness, respect, and thoughtfulness. As we learn to set realistic limits and boundaries we can begin to express ourselves in creative new ways.

Our desire for equality is changing in its expression: from doubt-filled, and therefore somewhat belligerent and defensive, to expressions of a firm inner conviction that we *are* equal and that it's unquestionably our right to express ourselves equally.

What are Limits and Boundries?

An emotionally independent woman knows and states her limits. She can stay within the boundaries of what she knows is good for her in both her personal and public life. Because she gives herself permission to be herself, she is able to say no without guilt, or at least with not enough guilt to keep her from doing what she knows is best for her health and well-being. Having emotional independence means we are no longer tied to the need for constant approval and are, therefore, not coerced by our need to please others into doing more than we feel comfortable doing.

Let's approach the idea of limits and boundaries through the backdoor. Have you ever found yourself allowing people to treat you in a way that you secretly found unacceptable? For instance, do you ever acquiesce to unkind, disrespectful treatment that makes you feel devalued? I came from a family where teasing was a way of relating for some of the members. I hated it and felt hurt each time I was teased. I didn't ask for the teasing to stop because I feared that setting a limit would make them tease me all the more or (oh, horrors!) cause them to reject and ignore me. Finally, as an adult, I was able to tell the teasers that being teased was not acceptable to me. Without any fuss at all, they stopped. When we are really solid in our belief that we don't need to submit to unacceptable treatment, and state our limit clearly, it will probably stop.

Whenever we receive unacceptable treatment in silent suffering, or whine and beg ineffectually to be treated better, we ignore our limits and permit others to invade the boundaries of our self-respect.

When others need something, do they always call on "good old you" and know you will come through even if you've just come home from ten days in intensive care? Letting people take advantage of you is not honoring your limits.

If we say yes when we're actually dying to say no, we aren't communicating our limits honestly, and we're setting ourselves up to feel resentful, hostile, and depressed. Women who do this tend to adopt one of two modus operandi, withdrawing from others or blowing their tops. Not being honest about our personal limits and boundaries creates feelings of betrayal, anger, defensiveness, and bewilderment not only toward others but also toward ourselves. In our hearts we probably know that we have allowed fear to keep us from standing up for ourselves, so when we repeatedly

19

allow our limits and boundaries to be trampled, we run the risk of losing respect for ourselves.

Learning to stand up for ourselves and honor our limits and boundaries involves, first, noticing when we're being taken advantage of; second, giving ourselves *permission* to have and to honor our limits and boundaries; and third, exploring and healing the fears that keep us living as a doormat. In order to have fair and open relationships with others, we must learn how to communicate our limits and boundaries honestly.

Giving Ourselves Away

Not respecting our limits and boundaries leads to giving ourselves away, that is, putting what we need and want below the needs and desires of those around us. Among the people you know, including yourself, who gets their wants and needs met most readily? Make an impromptu list of your acquaintances and their wants and needs, both tangible desires like a new car and a well-paying job, and intangibles such as receiving respect, being heard, and having opinions valued. Is there anyone on the list who always gets what they ask for? Are there some persons who are more than likely to get what they want? Where would you rate by comparison? If you'd be near the bottom, you're probably giving yourself away.

Maria lived for nineteen years with an emotionally abusive husband. She endured being put down privately and publicly and learned to "laugh it off." Having been raised a Catholic and holding staunch no-divorce views, she felt she had no choice but to accept her fate; thus, she gave herself away and came to loathe both herself and her husband.

We may give ourselves away in big chunks (not returning to school because that would inconvenience somebody) or small chunks (not speaking up when we're hurt or annoyed). Big or little, all chunks eventually add up to the equation that we are not living *our own* lives. Take a look at the following list of questions. If you can answer yes to any of them, you're probably giving yourself away in some areas:

1. Do you have self-limiting fears?
2. Are you often filling the wants and needs of others without having your own needs met?
3. Do you say yes when you'd like to say no?
4. Are decisions difficult for you?
5. Are your close relationships unsatisfying?
6. Do you lack self-confidence?
7. Are you your own worst critic?
8. Are you overtired much of the time?
9. Does your life have little joy and spontaneous laughter?

Women who give themselves away have a hard time making decisions because they're afraid of appearing stupid if they make a mistake. When I separated from my first husband, I needed to buy a car. I looked at several but felt unable to choose one. I asked my estranged husband for his advice—an okay thing to do if asking as an equal; but I considered his opinion more valuable than my own. My intuition was screaming, No, no, no!, but I ignored it and bought the car he chose.

That car and I were enemies from the very start. By not heeding my inner voice, I gave myself away—and got a car I could hardly live with. If I had had the courage to heed my inner voice and make the decision for myself, I would have come away feeling better about my integrity—and maybe I'd have gotten a better car!

Habitually feeling no but saying yes is a good indication we are giving ourselves away.

Saying "Yes" But Feeling "No"

Ever come away from the phone after having said yes to forty-eight dozen cookies for a Halloween party, the chairpersonship of two committees, and extra work hours that conflicted with personal plans?

Afterward, you feel you could cut out your tongue, die, or at least develop some highly contagious disease. Feeling like that means you've just given yourself away.

Saying yes when we feel no probably means we've been "should-ing" on ourselves. We're afraid that we aren't being nice enough when we say no or that people will dislike us for letting them down. Yet I've discovered that when I'm convinced I have a right to say no, and say it firmly, people accept it. They seem to get the message in direct proportion to how staunchly I hold the conviction. Replace your draining "should's" with empowering words like *can, want to, choose to,* or *will.*

A key method for having your no's heard is to choose one statement and stick with it:

You: I'm not able to chair this particular committee. I'm sorry.
They: Oh, please! I don't have anyone else I can call.
You: I know that's hard, but I just am not able to do it at this time of year.
They: I don't know what I'll do. I'm desperate.
You: It really is hard to organize this stuff, isn't it? I'm really sorry I'm not able to help you right now.

Notice that the "You" person in the scenario stuck to the statement, "I'm not able to" thereby honoring her limits and boundaries while expressing compassion for the other person's problem. "You" did not give herself away.

Before you say yes, take several deep breaths. Ask yourself if you're merely saying yes out of guilt or fear. Tell yourself that you have the right to choose. Pause! If you need time to consider your alternatives, take it, and return the phone call later. You don't have to let yourself be terrorized by other people's expectations of you.

The Terror Of Expectations

Unrealistic expectations can cause us to give ourselves away to such an extent that we end up feeling we are a tiny little nubbin of exhaustion without one iota of energy left to do the next task. That may sound melodramatic, but haven't we all pushed ourselves past our limits because we expected we could do it all—and perfectly? Or because we felt others expected perfection of us?

Your own expectations and the expectations of others can kill you emotionally. All of us—women, men, and children, young and old—have suffered under the tyranny of expectations. Didn't we expect our honeymoons to be romantic and idyllic? Few are.

I recently saw a scene from a play in which one of the characters gave a wonderful commentary on expectations; she was talking to a classmate at a high-school reunion and said, "I thought that once he and I got together things would change. That's what's written over the women's entrance to Hell: 'Things Will Change'."

So much of what we women expect is sheer fantasy. We expect to be able to make our families happy. (Our families, too, expect us to make them happy.) We expect ourselves to be unfailingly bright, cheerful, and healthy. We expect ourselves to be unchangingly attractive, always nurturing, and forever ready with wisdom and comfort. Unrealistic expectations such as these are exhausting, not to speak of terrifying and paralyzing.

One of the most crippling things we can do to ourselves is expect someone else to make us happy. Other people can only help to bring out what is already within us: the capacity to feel good about ourselves, to feel useful, to feel loved. When we feel unhappy and unfulfilled "because" of others, we can be sure we're giving ourselves away. We then need to take a long look at the beliefs and expectations we hold which are keeping us dependent on others.

Maria, the woman who was raised a Catholic and who was emotionally abused by her husband, woke up one morning and said, "Enough!" To save her life emotionally, she left her husband. Unfortunately, having taken so long to free herself from the rigid rules of her church and to realize that she had other choices, she was forced to leave her two children behind. Had she honored her limits and boundaries sooner, her marriage might have been salvaged; but so many years of swallowed pain and anger had created scars so deep that it was too late.

Notice that there's a delicate difference between asking for what we want and need, and expecting others to follow a hidden script we've written for them. Often, especially when two independent people are involved, there are going to be different ideas about how to live, work, and play. By adhering too rigidly to our own, interiorized picture of how things *should* be, we activate normal, healthy rebellion in the other person.

My husband and I had a fairy-tale romance; we met in Hawaii and courted across the Pacific. It was perfect—we were perfect, confident that we'd been sprinkled with fairy dust and that our relationship would be forever blissful. Of course, it wasn't. After we'd settled into an everyday routine, our expectations of unending bliss began to get in the way of our real lives.

As a novice marriage counselor with a divorce in my background, I felt I had a pretty realistic picture of what my new marriage should be. However, my husband's wants, needs, and images differed significantly from mine. It took me a long time and a lot of grieving to realize that I was smothering our relationship with my expectations. I was activating my husband's rebel personality with my it-has-to-be-this-way script. After a great deal of inner struggling, I was able to stop terrorizing both of us with my idealistic expectations.

A funny thing then happened: after a cooling-off period, when he trusted that I had really gotten off his back, he began to be the way I'd earlier demanded that he be. Since I'd released those expectations and found other ways to fulfill those needs, his change was much appreciated (the chocolate chips in the cookie of life), but was no longer necessary for my emotional survival.

As I found out, in even the most stable and caring relationships, there will be unmet expectations. I may expect a quiet evening of firelight and intimate sharing, and he may intend to watch basketball. We both may expect our kids for dinner, and they'll want to go have pizza with friends. We simply can't survive emotionally if we insist that every expectation be fulfilled. Life just isn't set up that way; so the healthiest response is to stay very flexible and not take it personally when our expectations aren't met.

The Superwoman Trap

Whatever women do they must do twice as well as men to be thought half as good. Luckily, this is not difficult.
-Charlotte Whitton

Being flexible and being a patsy aren't the same thing. One of the ways we give ourselves away is in trying to be everything to everybody: playing the omnipresent, omnicompetent Superwoman.

Superwoman's cape is lined with guilt and trimmed with fear. Fear that she won't live up to others' expectations, and guilt when she doesn't. The self-defined Superwoman can never fly; her expectations are rarely met, and even when they are, she merely replaces them with higher and ever-unattainable new ones.

I had a client who raised three children alone. She's remarried now and is raising a stepchild as well as three emotionally disturbed adopted siblings. She makes nearly all their clothes, cooks all the family's meals from scratch, balances a budget that would send chills up a contortionist's spine, and remains extremely active in her church. She used to get very upset when she occasionally felt unloving.

This woman comes from a background of trauma and deprivation which left her with deep emotional scars and her feet firmly caught in the Superwoman trap. She never felt that she compared favorably to other people and berated herself for a bewildering variety of real and imagined small failures. I used to get exhausted listening to her tell about just one of her adopted children and his deviant behavior.

Little by little, she was able to create a small sign to hang over her soul, at least some of the time:

Superwoman Doesn't Live Here Anymore!

Of course, women who are caught in the stranglehold of the Superwoman trap are often driven by economic necessity, as well as personal desire, to hold down a full-time job outside the home and a full-time job inside as well. Whether we are career women, at-home women, or both, we are often prodded mercilessly by an inner dragon to be perfect. As we find the courage to allow ourselves to be who we are—imperfect, but committed to improvement—we begin to untie the ropes that bind us to emotional dependence.

CHAPTER 3

Allowing
Ourselves
To Be Invaded

*Once a man is on hand, a woman tends
to stop believing in her own beliefs.*

-Colette Dowling

Many of us look outside ourselves for self-esteem—a contradiction in terms when you think about it. Asking others to mirror our value back to us, to keep us filled up with worth, inevitably leaves us feeling used and invaded. You also allow yourself to be invaded if: you constantly do for others and often resent that your own needs are not met; you doubt your ability to make decisions and therefore acquiesce whenever someone says, "No, no, I think you should (____)"; your children, mate, co-workers, and friends borrow from you without asking; or people feel free to use your time thoughtlessly.

We become vulnerable to invasion through fear: fear of rejection, imperfection, embarrassment, or confrontation. Because we fear other people's reactions, we allow them to violate our limits and boundaries. Fortunately, our physical and emotional responses tell us when someone has trespassed on our private selves, and we can learn to tune into those feelings and use them as valuable clues for maintaining reasonable limits.

Invasion brings feelings of being taken advantage of, of having to give up something. If one of my children goes into my bathroom and borrows my hairbrush without asking, I feel invaded, as if I've given up the right to have my things where and when I want them. The child has stepped past a boundary that has been clearly spelled out, and I feel angry and resentful.

When you've just settled into a warm bath after a hard day at work and the kids bang on the door for you to settle a disagreement, whether you'll be invaded or not will depend upon your reaction. If, because of a false sense of responsibility for their happiness, you leap out of the tub and rush to solve their problems, you've allowed them to invade you. I know women who say they never have a moment to themselves because of the demands of their jobs and families. One woman told me she constantly feels as if she's being "nibbled to death by ducks."

But it's not really outer circumstances that keep these women going at a killing pace; it's requirements they impose on themselves through their imprisonment in the Superwoman trap. While it's true that the demands on a woman to play many roles are stressful, we do have the right to make choices that put ourselves first. In fact, regularly giving ourselves permission to be first may actually help others to grow as well. If you don't bound from the tub at first call, your children will need to rely on their own resources to solve their dispute. As you assert your independence, they will have to find theirs, too.

Choosing to heal the fears that keep us emotionally dependent and believing we have no rights opens the door to honoring our limits and boundaries. When we no longer allow ourselves to be invaded we are well on our way to having the courage to be ourselves.

Footprints On Our Faces

When I was in high school, I gave my best friend the nickname "Footprint" because she allowed her boyfriend to walk all over her. I'm sure I deserved the name, too, for the way I behaved with some of the boys I dated. My friend and I felt vaguely uncomfortable and powerless as doormats, but this was the 1950s, when girls were encouraged to cater to boys and, in many respects, times haven't changed all that much.

I remember reading a series of little YWCA books on dating, menstruating, and the art of making a proper phone call. The booklet on dating actually said that in order to be popular (that summit of adolescent values!), a girl should let the boy talk about himself. The booklet said to ask the boy leading questions that would get him started talking about topics of interest to him. To build a boy's interest in me, I was to feign interest in cars and sports or whatever that particular boy liked.

Surely those books had been reprinted from volumes discovered in some moldy Victorian attic! I remember thinking, Isn't that a stupid game? What if there's a subject I'd like to talk about? My doubts manifested themselves in an interesting way; I developed a chronic frog in my throat; especially when out on a date, I felt that I would choke at any minute. Often I'd need to excuse myself to find a private place to hack and cough. I was literally choking on the sincere words I held back and the game-like words I spoke. More basically, I was choking on the underlying message from those how-to-get-along-with-boys suggestions: You aren't as important as they are. I carried that semi-hidden belief that I was second-rate with me into adulthood. I also carried my throat frog.

Several years ago I filled in an assertiveness inventory in a magazine. Since I already had my master's in psychology, and had been through a very growth-producing divorce, and felt I'd made great progress in developing self-esteem. I was shocked and angered when I tested fairly assertive in all areas except in my relations with the men I loved, including my two sons.

In fact, I had to admit that I was acting out a lingering assumption that men are better, deserve to be listened to more than women, and would probably leave me if I didn't take a backseat to them in most matters. I allowed men to invade me by firmly planting their tennies on my face. *Croak!* Significantly, my need to clear my throat was a family joke and, I learned later, a constant irritation to my husband.

I decided to do something about it. I began to assert myself with men, even with the men I loved. I ferreted out my hidden attitudes of subservience and stopped giving myself away. The process was not easy and required the help of a good therapist, supportive friends, clients, and my own stick-to-itiveness.

The frog in my throat, which had been with me constantly for twenty-eight years, disappeared. Now, if I begin to choke and croak, I look for ways in which I've slipped and allowed myself to be invaded. Froggie has become an important teacher.

Roles To Conquer The Invader

One of the primary urges people need to fulfill in their lives is the desire to have and to express their personal power. Thus, when we feel invaded or taken advantage of, we immediately seek ways to defeat the threatening invader. Since society hasn't encouraged women to develop their power (it isn't feminine, you know), we have adopted secret and dishonest means of having and using power. The trouble with deviousness, though, is that in the long run, everyone who uses it loses.

Here are some of the secret negative strategies women have adopted:

Mother

There are just three periods in our lives when we need to be mothered: in infancy, in senility, and when ill. The rest of the time, no matter who we are, we need to develop our own inner capacity to be strong and take care of ourselves. Yet women have chosen to mother men and other women, despite the thoroughly proven fact that an inappropriate motherly attitude means death to romantic love and the love between equal marriage partners, as well as to friendship.

I often find myself having to tell my women clients to "monitor their Mom-isms." A Mom-ism expresses itself in ways as trivial as telling a driver where to park: "Why don't you park by the bank?" You may say that this is just being helpful, but in the driver's mind it most likely will be interpreted as patronizing, as being unnecessarily coddling, and as being treated like a stupid, incapable child. No one enjoys being told that he or she can't perform simple tasks such as deciding where to park a car. Of course, if help is asked for, that's different.

Another Mom-ism is nagging. When we feel the need to remind and reproach, we are nagging: "Have you done (___) yet?" "You shouldn't go out with only that light sweater! You'll catch your death of cold." "How many times do I have to tell you to do (whatever)?!" People soon learn to turn a deaf ear, or a rebellious back, to nagging.

To be fair, there's another side to the Mom-ism coin: the man's tendency to play Little Boy in an effort to get a woman to adopt the mother role, take care of him and fulfill him inwardly. But you can stop your part. It may leave teeth marks on your tongue, but if you want to save your relationships with your mate, children, friends, and co-workers, stop being everybody's mom.

Monitor your Mom-isms. They don't help you or anyone

else; rather, they destroy your freedom and others' self-esteem. To the extent you feel the need to mother another adult, you will also shoulder his or her responsibility. If you are carrying all the responsibility in a relationship, why should the other person even attempt to carry his own? It's interesting that the Chinese symbols for *attachment* and *mother* when combined spell *poison*. When we attach ourselves to the role of mother, usurping others' right to learn from their own mistakes, we poison the relationship between us.

Martyr/Victim

We all know people who play martyr/victim roles, people who go around sighing: "Poor me!"; "If only they had . . ."; "Whatever you want . . . (sigh)"; "I don't care . . . (sigh)"; "It's not important how I feel . . . (sigh)." We learn these roles. We see our mothers and grandmothers manipulating others with them. But actually, victims feel powerless and perceive themselves to be ruled by others' actions and judgments. The martyr/victim role is incredibly controlling because it evokes guilt.

People who play the victim role were often victimized in childhood, when they were helpless. As adults, they still feel powerless in their world, and ruled by others' actions and opinions. A perpetual victim never has to take responsibility for her own life because everything that happens is obviously someone else's fault. The victim personifies an emotionally dependent person because she's a captive of her reactions rather than the captain of her actions. Grown-up victims fill their lives with impossible "should's" and "have-to's," by which they dwell on their failures and beat themselves up continuously over their believed ineffectualness.

Alicia's father died when she was very young and she felt abandoned by him. Her mother was unstable and became more so after her husband's death. Being a "good" girl, Alicia took on the role of parent to her mother, and through the years preceding her mother's suicide, felt victimized by her situation. She had given up her childhood to her mother's emotional dependence. Alicia believed that no matter how much she loved, those she loved would leave her. She wanted and needed love herself but, entrenched in the victim role, she had a series of relationships with men who either abandoned her emotionally or invaded every corner of her life. Alicia's son also victimized her, quite literally, with threats of murder and suicide.

She was trapped in her internal litany: I'm so helpless; why don't they change? But until Alicia realizes that she is responsible for recasting herself in the role of victim, she will continue to allow herself to be invaded. Until she begins to honor her limits and boundaries and stand up for her rights, she will continue to live a helplessly restricted life.

Alicia is a "Yes, but..." person, so solidified in her identity as victim that she responds to every positive suggestion with "Yes, but..." followed by the reason why she can't be free of whatever person or situation is currently victimizing her. If I suggest that it might be good for her self-image, bank account, and marriage to get a different job, she says, "Yes, but there are no jobs," or, "Yes, but I don't have up-to-date skills." When told that it's essential that she have therapy to heal and release her old resentments and thought patterns, she says, "Yes, but it would be so hard," or, "Yes, but there aren't any good therapists." She alone is keeping herself stuck in her unhappy victim role, with her "Yes, but"-ting.

The only way to get out of the victim role is to choose to take personal responsibility for your life as it is now and as it can be. Accepting responsibility may very well require the help of a therapist and/or honest friend who can lovingly expose the way you use the victim role and its consequences in your life.

I once had a client who said, "Martyrdom is for emergencies only!" I love that statement for the depth of truth in it. We use martyrdom to get what we want from others, to bludgeon them into submission through guilt. When manipulating others, we martyrs can feel so chaste, noble, long-suffering, and self-righteous. But we can also feel incredibly lonely.

My grandmother was a grand mistress of martyrdom and victimization. No matter what anyone did for her, it wasn't enough. Being around her was an experience of continuous guilt and consequently we avoided her as much as possible.

No one feels comfortable listening while a martyr whines about all the ways we're responsible for her health, happiness, and self-esteem, and how we've all failed. By fostering guilt in others the martyr contaminates herself and creates the very situation she fears: rejection, loss of love, isolation.

These thoughts and others like them are sure tipoffs that you're playing the martyr: After all I've done for them! or, I gave him the best years of my life, and now look at what he's given me in return! or, If only the children would call once in a while.

Margaret, a class-A martyr, told me, "The children never call me . . . (sigh)." (Martyrs sigh a lot.) When I asked if she ever called them, she replied that she didn't for fear they'd feel she was intruding.

Her kids were in a bind. They were supposed to read Mom's mind, and they were guilty if they didn't. Moreover, they'd spent a lifetime getting wise to her martyrdom so they didn't particularly care to call her up for yet another load of guilt. Therefore Margaret found herself alone a lot until she learned to take responsibility for conveying what she wanted and needed without punishing others with guilt.

Invalid

There are people whom we would call invalids who are courageous beyond belief, who use their physical limitations to grow and stretch their intellectual and spiritual boundaries enormously, and, by the very way they handle pain, are inspirations to us. But the invalid I am referring to here is the woman who uses illness—real or imagined—to escape from life or to manipulate others. Who can invade us if we're always in ill health? No one can expect us to give ourselves away. No one can refuse to grant our needs and desires when we can't take care of ourselves.

Sonya was strong as a horse while her five children were young and needed her constant care. However, as her kids began to grow up, branch out and have lives of their own, she began to develop ill health. As each child prepared to leave home, Sonya's health failed more dramatically. Doctors were mystified because they could find no cause for her distress.

I met Sonya through her youngest child, Mattie, who had come to therapy to help assuage her guilt over leaving home and abandoning her "ill and helpless" mother. The three of us met together for several sessions in which Sonya, a very service oriented person, courageously uncovered her unconscious belief that her life was as good as over when her mother role terminated its daily function. Her body was following her subconscious instructions and shutting down as each child left.

Sonya was able to grasp and change what she was doing, begin to redefine her life, and choose different ways to serve. She learned more about her own unconscious process and is now a very healthy and active woman who provides a safe house for battered women and their children.

Sonya's invalid role was unconscious; Amelia's is not. Anytime Amelia's family tries to disagree with her, she has an asthma attack and must take to her bed where they can hear her gasping for breath because of what "they have said and done." In order to avoid the guilt of provoking attacks, her family avoids Amelia whenever possible.

Being chronically sick is powerful. True, little is expected of us . . . but look at the price we pay! When we're sick, our freedom is severely limited. Adopting the invalid role is invalid!

Bitch

A man can be called ruthless if he bombs a country to oblivion. A woman can be called ruthless if she puts you on hold.
　　　-Gloria Steinem

Many traditionally minded men (and women) will label you "bitch" if you're assertive and speak up for yourself. That is best ignored. But some women deserve the title because they use bitchiness to relieve their pent-up frustration at giving themselves away and being invaded in various other ways. They nag, gripe, use toxic humor to put people down, criticize, and, secretly, they weep.

Being bitchy isn't much fun for the bitch or the bitchee. Bitchiness is generally the result of unspoken rage. It never works as a long-term solution because it corrodes your self-esteem and alienates others.

Adrienne used to nag her husband when he came home late, grumble about him to her friends, and gripe when he didn't do things he'd promised. When they came in for counseling, she was just as down on herself as on him.

They were locked in a deadly stalemate: she felt neglected and deserted so she took on the role of bitch, admonishing and nagging, explaining and raving, crying and raging. He played the role of martyr and penitent little boy—passively agreeing with everything she said, then aggressively doing exactly what he wanted.

Adrienne was willing to look at her underlying reasons for adopting the bitch role and to stop it, but her husband wouldn't give up his part of the game, and they eventually divorced. She's generally happy now, though she remembers her marriage with sadness. She's no longer bitchy, and she loves the experience of taking charge of her life. Her relationships are exciting and mutually supportive. Her husband has moved on, to a woman who's even more demanding of him than Adrienne was. Adrienne broke the pattern; he did not.

If you react to frustration by feeling like a powerless little terrier, snarling and ripping at a knotted sock, chances are you're playing the bitch. Find out what's frustrating you. How are you allowing yourself to be invaded? Do you feel you've given so much of yourself away that there's nothing left? Women who resort to bitchiness generally aren't really mean—they're scared, and they long for honest, mutually independent relationships.

Girl-Woman

Women who play girl-woman are afraid, too, but they take the opposite tack from the bitch. A girl-woman needs to be cared for and protected, fathered and told what to do. Somewhere along the way these women have made the assumption that they aren't lovable unless they're "less than." They may have received the idea that they're incapable of taking care of themselves from overprotective parents who didn't allow them to make decisions—including mistakes—and who taught them that if they wanted to get through life, they'd better find someone to take care of them.

Beth, a tiny, sweet, pretty woman, who was in one of our

groups, talked in a soft little-girl voice and said that her husband didn't "let" her do many things. He wouldn't let her have a room in their house in which to paint, although he had both a study and hobby room of his own. She was very concerned that being in the group would make him angry. I said, "How old are you, Beth?" She replied, "Forty-six." After I asked her the question two more times, she looked up out of lowered eyes and giggled, "Sixteen." She had met her husband when she was sixteen, and there she had frozen, giving away her adulthood in order to hold his love, or so she believed. She felt invaded, resentful, and fearful. She was afraid that if she grew up, he wouldn't love her anymore.

I saw her just the other day. She speaks in an assured, adult manner, works as an administrator for a retirement facility, and is pursuing a graduate degree in gerontology, having designed the course of study herself. She's very happy with her husband. I asked her how old she was, and she replied proudly, "Forty-eight. And my husband likes me better this way!" As it turned out, her husband had felt burdened by her continuous need to be parented and he welcomed an equal relationship, though not without some initial resistance.

When you look inside yourself, do you find the uncomfortable and sabotaging feelings of mother, martyr-victim, invalid, bitch, or girl-woman? It can be scary to look honestly at our own behavior, but we can take comfort in the fact that virtually everyone who does it finds many things that need to be changed, and we all have the capacity to change ourselves for the better.

When we change, our relationships also begin to change. It is impossible for a relationship to remain the same when one of the persons involved alters his or her behavior. Facing the fear of change and acting in spite of it creates freedom. We can even use the greater fear of remaining in our painful ruts to impel ourselves into action. Frequently, the other people in our lives are relieved when we stop giving ourselves away.

CHAPTER 4

The Leveled Life

*It is not the end of the physical body
that should worry us. Rather, our
concern must be to live while
we're alive—to release our inner selves
from the spiritual death that comes
with living behind a facade designed to
conform to external definitions of
who and what we are.*

-Elisabeth Kubler-Ross

Women who are emotionally dependent often carry around an unspoken feeling that they're somehow missing out on life, that life is passing them by. Life, which had promised to be so exciting, full of joy and surprises, has turned out to be as level and barren as the salt flats. In fact, if life feels flat, it probably means we're living someone else's definition of our life and haven't taken the risk to find out who *we* are and what *we* want.

One of the biggest words in a flat, leveled life is "If": If only I'd . . . If only I hadn't . . . If only they. . . If only I'd known . . . If only, if only, if only . . .

"If" comes from Ignorance teamed with Fear: ignorance of possibilities in life, and fear of taking the risks involved in seizing those possibilities and being who we authentically are.

Children are natural-born risk-takers. They move out into the world and toward others with their arms wide open. For children, life is full of mountains and valleys waiting to be explored. There's nothing level about the life of a healthy, spontaneous child: one moment she'll be rolling around in a fit of glee; the next moment, she's grabbing aggressively for her doll and sobbing.

When we see a child acting level and flat, we take her temperature. Why, then, do we feel it's okay for *us* to ooze through life on a boring, uniform plane? What, after all, is okay about a life that's safe but lacks wonder, enthusiasm, anger, and joy? What's normal about living from a place within ourselves that knows no spontaneous gratitude, sense of rightness, and harmony with the scheme of things?

Often we fall into the habit of living blah lives so gradually that we aren't aware of how flat and bland our lives have become. When my first husband left me, I realized how level my life was. When the shock wore off, I experienced an explosion of emotions. I'd be low, then I'd skyrocket in a frenzy of rage and desire for revenge. I'd be thinking of suicide, then I'd be giddy with fantasies about the possibilities that lay open before me.

During the years it took to heal those wounds, I experienced the widest range of feelings that I'd had since I was a teenager. I became aware of how painful my life was because of its flatness, and I decided to do something about it. One of my first, fleeting reactions was: I'm never going to let myself be hurt like this again. Never, never, never! To protect myself, I locked myself up in an emotional bubble-dome, out of reach and invulnerable. But that didn't last long because I soon began to understand my own role in the breakup: how, in my emotional dependence, I had leveled my own life.

During that first marriage, I was unwilling to be aware of what was going on inside of me. It was simply too scary. As a defense mechanism, I became funny on the outside, covertly and ineffectually venting my anger by telling funny but barbed stories. Later, when I was able to see my actions without flinching, but instead with love and forgiveness, I chose to act differently. I took back my promise never to be hurt again and replaced it with two affirmations that I still live by.

The first was: *I choose to really live.* For me, that m
commitment to risk-taking and to experiencing *all o.* ıny
feelings, whether joyous, painful, or indifferent. I had tried to
avoid pain all my life; now I was learning that in order to live
I had to embrace life's whole package: the pain as well as the
joy—the entire gamut of my emotions. It wasn't a decision I
made lightly or easily.

I was helped immensely by this passage from Kahil
Gibran's *The Prophet*:

> *Your joy is your sorrow unmasked*
> *And the selfsame well from which your laughter rises*
>   *was oftentimes filled with your tears*
> *And how else can it be?*
> *The deeper that sorrow carves into your being,*
>   *the more joy you can contain.*

My second affirmation was: *I will never give myself away
again.* Giving yourself away depletes you until you no longer
feel there is a you. Instead, I decided to explore my boundaries. What did I want to do with my life? Whom did I want to
do it with? What behavior was acceptable to me? What could
I do to increase my independence and my ability to love
others? How could I be a supportive yet firm parent? What
did I need to heal in order to resist the temptation to give
myself away again?

The Higher You Go, The Farther You'll Fall

Many of us hold the image that life is a pie. It's dished out
in large and small pieces and when it's gone, it's gone. Therefore, we don't tempt the gods by asking for too much; after all,
if we ask for more than our share, we're just begging to be
disappointed. We are often trained to believe that the higher

you go, the farther you'll fall.

When we were children, and the joy of risking and stretching was still natural to us, we were warned:

- *Don't get too excited.*
- *Remember, there are only two spots on the cheerleading squad, and 14 girls trying out for them.*
- *Don't get your heart set on it.*
- *You'll cry as hard tomorrow as you laugh today.*
- *Don't expect too much from (____) (marriage is a good fill-in for that one!).*
- *Life is hard.*
- *Don't rock the boat.*

What are the underlying messages behind such statements?

Maybe some of these:
- *It's dangerous to risk.*
- *It's dangerous to hope, to be happy, to expect life to be good and fulfilling.*
- *There isn't ever enough to go around.*
- *Give up your childlike awe and wonder.*

I know a woman whose favorite statement is: Life is hard and then you die. What's your image of a woman whose life is determined by such a statement? Is she constantly threatened by scarcity? Yes. Does she cling to the old because risk-taking is scary? Yes. This woman believes that life is hard, and so for her it jolly well is. She gets what she believes life will give her.

If you're one of the older children in your family, can you remember the birth of your first sibling? I do. I remember being both excited and scared. Would my parents have enough love for both of us? They assured me they would, so

I began to look forward to my baby. Then my grandmother gave me this input, which was all too easy for seven-year-old to take to heart: "Even though your mother and daddy will now have someone they love more than you, I'll still love you." You can imagine how I welcomed my baby sister after that—with open hostility. Because I believed I'd be unloved, I felt unloved. I *was* loved, but for many crucial years I was unable to feel it; and this scarcity of feeling loved contributed much toward the leveling of my life in adulthood. It was only with the loving help of friends, my mother, and therapy that I was eventually healed.

Linda's family gave her the message that she must *do it right or don't do it at all!* She was never given permission to learn, risk, and experiment, so she developed a pattern she called "slip 'n' quit." Since nobody does things right the first time, and since she had never been encouraged to make mistakes and therefore had no support system to buoy her up while her life jacket was in for repairs, she took up a whole series of things in which she slipped and quit, including ice skating and ballet.

Linda was afraid to climb higher for fear of falling farther. Her habit of slipping and quitting fostered a fear of trying, so she settled for less and less, shedding dreams almost before she was fully conscious of them. Her life became level.

Linda's story has a happy ending: as she became aware of her limiting pattern, she was able to give herself permission to do it even if she did it wrong. Linda is becoming a loving parent to herself and is gradually acquiring more and more courage to be who she really is. I saw her recently, and she was glowing with enthusiasm about a new job and the overflow of energy she felt for the job as well as for other areas of her life. She told me she still slipped, but that she had been able to promise herself not to quit.

Safe But Sorry

When we settle for less in order to feel safe, we always feel sorry. If we compromise our dreams, limiting ourselves with negative ideas gleaned in childhood or adulthood; if we accept that it's useless to ask for what we want and need; if we believe lack is safer than abundance, our lives will close around us like a warm, safe but suffocating blanket.

There are few greater disappointments than being forced to admit that our lives have been a series of compromises that have left us feeling dull and out of touch with our dreams. My dad used to tell me when I was feeling low, "It's just one of those little valleys on the highway of life." I didn't much appreciate the statement then, but I've since come to understand how right he was. If we are to enjoy the "high ways" of life, we need to learn from and grow in the valleys.

We do need security, but security can be purchased at too high a price. Security obtained at the expense of exhilarating, creative growth and change merely strangles us. Surely the caterpillar feels secure in its cocoon but when it emerges, it needs to unfold its wings and risk flight.

Give up your need to be safe but sorry. Resolve your grief over the leveling of your life by choosing to take flight. Have the courage to **SOAR: Stretch Out And Risk.** You *can* do it.

You already have the courage you need to grow beyond emotional dependence. The very act of reading this book, which is full of challenges to grow and change, is courageous. And now we'll look at the road map that I find extremely helpful as I continue my journey toward having the courage to be who I am.

CHAPTER 5

Getting There: A Road Map

We're not yet where we're going but we're not still where we were.

-Natasha Jasefowitz

*A*re you sitting beside your life's road waiting for someone to come along and give you a ride? Someone to take you on *their* trip? We women were taught to wait patiently for life. Some of our best tour guides were Doris Day and Rock Hudson, Ozzy and Harriet Nelson, TV programs such as "Father Knows Best"—and our own mothers.

Who ever heard of a damsel rescuing a knight in distress? We may do it all the time, but we were taught to act as if someone else were in the driver's seat of our life. It doesn't work! The journey is our own. We need to chart our own course and make our own decisions in order to be true to who we really are.

No matter where we're going—to the supermarket, to work, to Europe, to a career, to marriage—we need maps to show us how to get to our destination. As women who seek to be free of emotional dependence, we, too, need road maps. This book is designed to provide you with many maps that have helped me and my clients and friends find our way to greater inner freedom. I encourage you to use these maps gently and tolerantly.

Road maps generally contain a large, overall map, plus smaller maps of the cities in the area. I'll now show you the "big map" for the rest of this book, which I call:

The Three-A Map

AWARENESS: Become *aware* of your feelings. Inner awareness is the beginning of outer change.

ACKNOWLEDGMENT: *Tell* a trusted friend or counselor about your awareness.

ACCEPTANCE: *Honor* where you are and what you are feeling. Give yourself a break! You're okay as you are, even as you seek to change!

The first and most basic step for any change or growth, no matter how small, is to know what we feel, how we think, and how we would like to alter our lives. In others words, we first need to be aware of where we are and where we want to go. Then we need to acknowledge where we are to someone else. Acknowledgment keeps us honest and helps us break out of denial. When we realistically acknowledge what we have become aware of to ourselves and to a trusted friend, we are more likely to move toward our destination. Finally, acceptance acts as our fuel, propelling us out of limiting patterns, energizing us for needed change.

Let's look at these three steps in more detail.

Awareness

All change begins with awareness. Becoming aware of what we're thinking and, even more important, what we're feeling, enables us to work with and change our attitudes and actions. If we're not aware of what we're feeling, the feeling will become our master. When we suppress or repress an emotion, we lose control over how we express it, even though we *will* express it. A repressed or suppressed emotion builds up power until it can't be held in anymore, and most likely we'll express it in destructive ways. But when we become aware of our feelings early in the process, we can *choose* how to express them constructively.

This is not to say that it's easy to become aware of our feelings. Many of us spend our entire lives trying to please others without ever thinking about what we want or need. Consider this poem by Roseanne, a career person with two children, a husband, and a difficult live-in father-in-law:

Saturday

The family has gone on an outing,
Responsibilities I've put on the shelf.
This Saturday I have been counting
On spending some time on myself.

But life is full of vexation.
That fact should have given me a clue
To expect unexpected complications
... I've forgotten what I like to do!

Roseanne had lost herself in constantly pleasing others. She felt depressed because she had repressed her own, unfulfilled needs. When she began to see that she, too, had rights, that she did not have to sacrifice herself on the altar of her family and her job, she also became aware of what she wanted and needed. In therapy she began to detach herself from the old, burdening sense of responsibility for the lives of all the people around her. Now, she feels free to make a life for herself and, consequently, feels more loving toward her family.

Warning! As you begin to honor your feelings and needs, you may find others labeling you as selfish, or you may find yourself feeling selfish. Most of us were taught to think of others first. Thus initially it will feel strange and even self-indulgent not to deny your own feelings, wants, and needs. But if you remember that the suppression of these needs and desires causes more harm to you and your loved ones, it should help you have the courage to identify your feelings.

Another obstacle to greater awareness is the fact that un-awareness pays off in short-term ways by letting us ignore pain and anger. When Ruth was a child, her mother beat her when she misbehaved or spoke out of turn. Ruth learned to turn off emotionally, to become as invisible as possible, to detach herself from people and avoid intimate relationships. As a child, those were survival skills; as an adult, they give her great pain.

Ruth became so good at detaching herself from her feelings that she actually did not feel the pain of those beatings. Today, the little girl inside her, whom she still tries desperately to protect, is afraid to get too close to people. As a result, Ruth feels terribly isolated and lonely. What helped her survive in the past keeps her separated in the present.

Many of the choices we made when we were young were wise at the time. In learning to deal with our fears in new and more creative ways, we should be very patient and gentle with ourselves. It's not at all appropriate to feel guilty for childhood patterns that may have helped us survive. After all, when we made those early decisions, we were doing the very best we could. And, in many cases, it was truly heroic!

Now, however, we can allow ourselves to truly think and feel what is ours to know and experience. Simply being aware that "Hey, I don't like it when she says that to me" can be very liberating emotionally. Freedom starts with knowing how we feel.

Awareness begins with an inner inquiry that goes something like this: What am I feeling? When did it start? Where does my body hold it in the form of tension? Is it a familiar

56

feeling? How is this feeling limiting me? What is scaring me?

Inner dialogue helps us stop blaming circumstances and other people for the hurts and disappointments in our lives. It allows us to assume responsibility for our own reactions. As we talk things over with ourselves, we'll become more and more able to sit in the driver's seat of our lives.

The key is always to bring the responsibility back to ourselves. We may not be able to change events, but we can change our reaction to them. What am I doing? Why? Why am I saying this? How am I setting this situation up?

The dialogue must be conducted gently. If you blame and verbally abuse yourself for problems and situations, you'll drown yourself in guilt, which will keep you from moving *through* uncomfortable feelings. Don't use responsibility as an excuse for beating yourself up emotionally. If you start to feel guilty, ask yourself, Just who is demanding that I feel badly? You'll probably run across an internalized critical-parent voice.

Frequently, when we use inner dialogue, the person we're talking with is our inner, vulnerable child. If we're not careful to be very understanding and tolerant, our inner child will hide, and we won't be able to understand the choices she's making that are limiting us as adults.

Becoming aware of feelings is like shining a light in the closet to make all the bogeymen and goblins run away. You may think, Well, it's easy for you to talk about inner dialogue, but I've got so much junk buried away that if I open the door, it'll completely overwhelm me. But that's why you're reading this book: because it gives you practical tools for dealing with your fears in manageable doses.

In my work with women, I've discovered that we seem to have an inner control mechanism that doles out just as many slimy toads and beasties as we can handle at a given time. The fear of being overwhelmed can hinder us by over encouraging us to *under*whelm ourselves and avoid facing our difficult feelings.

If you sense that you have hidden fears that threaten to erupt with volcanic force, by all means see a therapist immediately before you begin to work on your own. Some people have repressed fears that can only be healed with patient professional help.

At times you may need a strong, objective hand to hold. But much of the time, we can parcel out our inner discoveries in manageable, bite-sized pieces.

Acknowledgment

The next step towards change is acting on our awareness. Fully acknowledging our new-found realization helps us reconnect with others. Fearful secrets separate us from people. They are like mushrooms . . . put them in a dark place, cover liberally with manure, and they will "mushroom!"

Honestly and gently acknowledging our feelings and beliefs breaks the isolation and loneliness in which we live. We all need to feel understood and connected to others. In a climate of nonjudgmental love, we can truly become who we are meant to be.

There are many styles of acknowledging. My own style is to talk openly and honestly about my fears and the dark, nasty feelings I have inside of me. I process my feelings more quickly and efficiently when I verbalize them. If my feelings are out in the open, verbally hanging in the atmosphere, I can sort them out, understand them, and change them. Without the understanding of others, it takes me much longer to sort through my feelings. When understanding ears are scarce, I use my journal to talk to myself.

My internal process works best when it's externalized. Unexpressed, my feelings grab me by the neck and strangle me. It has been absolutely essential for me, in developing the courage to be myself, to find people who will hear me without judgment, and who will know with me that "this, too, shall pass." I sort as I talk, but other people may have different methods.

Become aware of your most natural and comfortable way of acknowledging. What helps you to move toward being really you? Is writing down how you feel helpful? Talking to yourself in the car? Be flexible: experiment with what works and what doesn't. Develop a style that is right for you.

At some point, it'll be important to acknowledge to someone other than yourself. It'll help reinforce your awareness, and experiencing the acceptance of another human being will foster your own self-acceptance.

Too often, we create limiting feelings by speaking to ourselves in a judgmental, no-win voice: You should; you must; you shouldn't. Such words activate an internal response: I won't! I can't! To resolve this kind of internal civil war, use words such as *could, choose to, want to," can, will,* and *will not.* This may seem like an overly simplistic technique, but it's not. Words such as *should* and *have to* imply that you have no power to choose in the matter. *Will* and *choose to* are words that free you to make conscious choices.

Have you ever said, "I feel sad," only to have someone retort sternly, "You shouldn't feel that way!" It stopped the conversation, didn't it? The connection with the other person was broken. Choose well the persons with whom you share your innermost feelings. You have a right to have your feelings, whatever they are. Painful feelings can be transmuted and healed only in a safe, accepting environment.

Learn to be a trusted friend yourself, and find friends and therapists whom you feel you can trust. Use your intuition in making these choices. You can only be honest in exploring your feelings if you don't fear the response of others.

When we're told we "shouldn't" feel sad or lonely or whatever, we will hesitate to open up again. And wisely so! We need and deserve to be treated with tenderness, respect, and understanding. As we heal and grow, it is best for us to reveal ourselves only to those who can accept our acknowledgment gently.

So share your secrets only with someone who will honor you by listening nonjudgmentally. As we talk to a trusted friend about our real and imagined shortcomings and our struggles to improve, we learn to forgive ourselves.

Acceptance

Do your best, even if you make apparent mistakes. How are you to judge if they are mistakes? You can only obey the higher urge which inclines you to contribute the best that you have to the service of the community of men [women] and angels. Thus, you shall be an evergrowing channel for the light.

-White Eagle

The third part of the road map is acceptance. After you become aware of feelings and thoughts and acknowledge them, you need to accept them in order to move through them.

Remember, feelings are neither right nor wrong—they just *are*. When you can accept your feelings just as they are, you'll be able to risk being honest outwardly. If you criticize and judge yourself for your feelings, you'll close down, hide, and relate less honestly to yourself and others.

Who likes to be browbeaten? How many times have you said, "I know it's so stupid, but I feel . . . ." or, "I know it's awful, but I feel like . . . ." or (one of my old favorites), "Oh, you dummy! How stupid can you be?" If our feelings are

always greeted by this kind of unloving, condemning dia-
tribe, it's no wonder we don't want to express them!

We can free ourselves from old rules about right and
wrong and from judgmental self-talk. My own self-talk used
to be excruciating. For instance, if I didn't like someone, I'd
berate myself with such wonderful put-downs as: Who are
you not to like her? You're not so swift yourself! or You are
only really a nice person if you love everyone.

Now, when I have such feelings, I look at them closely,
check to see if there's a lesson I need to learn, confide in a
friend if possible, and then tell myself something like: It's
okay, Toots. You don't have to like everybody.

Accept your feelings exactly as they are. When you do,
you'll provide an inner climate that's conducive to growth
and change. With acceptance, you no longer need to hide or
pretend. You can speak out and bring the secrets into the open
to be transformed. Acceptance nurtures, and nurturing allows you to flower into the beautiful blossom you were meant
to be.

Honor where you are and what you are feeling. Then if
you choose, you can move on to something different. Give
yourself a break! You're okay, and you're on the road to being
okay-er.

Accepting yourself just as you are is an act of forgiveness:
you forgiving you. Forgiving yourself also creates a mood in
which you find it easier to forgive and accept others.

An excellent way to foster forgiveness and acceptance is
visualization. Think about something you dislike about
yourself or something you wish you hadn't done. Say to
yourself: I did the best I knew how at the time; I am now
willing to forgive myself. Visualize yourself putting whatever you regret into a basket attached to a beautiful helium
balloon. Now take a deep breath and watch the balloon and

basket float away. Let it go! Throughout your day, repeat the visualization. Tell yourself that you are now willing to release guilt and forgive yourself. Don't expect to have instantaneous feelings of inner freedom and peace. Things held in for a long period take time to be cleansed. Be gentle and patient with yourself, and with time, it will change.

Julie's story exemplifies the power of the Three-A Map. Julie's mother was critical and abusive. In her therapy sessions with me, Julie *became aware* that she was trying to give me all the right answers, in order to avoid any possibility of my criticizing and judging her. She was trying too hard to please me (a mother figure) and be accepted by me. Later, she *acknowledged* this awareness to a personal friend, and they both *accepted* it without judgment.

In her next session with me, Julie spoke from such an honest place within herself, and it felt so completely natural to her, that she simply forgot to tell me about her new insight. At the end of our session, she realized that she was no longer trying to please me by saying all the right things. She then told me how using the Three-A Map had freed her from her initial fear of me.

As Julie's story shows, sometimes all it takes to change a behavior pattern is to *see* it and *say* it. Remember, acceptance of what you see and say is absolutely essential because only after you've accepted it can you move onward to alter whatever is limiting your freedom. Only then will you experience the inner feelings of authenticity that we all crave.

Being yourself is your birthright. You have all the tools within you to enable you to express yourself and your potential without being limited by fear.

Part Two

Facing The
Dragons
In The Dungeon

CHAPTER 6

Natural
And Learned
Fears

*Woman is buffeted by circumstances so
long as she believes herself to be
the creature of outside conditions, but
when she realizes that she is a
creative power, and that she may
command the hidden soil and seeds of her
being out of which circumstances
grow, she then becomes the rightful
master of herself.*

-James Allen

We are naturally curious but not naturally fearful. A baby is born with only two natural fears: fear of falling and fear of loud noises. When a baby is about to fall or hears a loud noise, it immediately goes into a fear response, inhaling sharply and stiffening. This initial physical reaction is followed by panicked crying. As adults, we still experience these primal, natural fears. *All* other fears, including fear of death, are learned.

Our culture, our families, and our governments use fear to control us. Fear can be a useful and beneficial means of instruction; but too often it's applied inappropriately, and we're conditioned to unhealthy fearfulness. We come out of childhood wearing the yoke of our family's and society's unresolved anxieties such as the fear of failure, embarrassment, appearing ignorant, and not being as good as the Joneses. In time we make their fears our own.

> *How does fear, or other emotion come about? We humans tend to believe that fear is created by the approach of the fearsome thing—the snake creeping towards us. But actually the small child tends to be curious rather than frightened by*

such things, until conditioned by the mother's
gasp and frantic reaction. Thereafter the emotion
of fear arises in the child when a snake
approaches. But it is not created by the snake.
It is created by the connection made in our mind.
It is caused by what we tell ourselves about
snakes.
                                    -Elizabeth Gawain

My mother was deathly afraid of dogs. She never ex-
pressly told me to fear dogs, but as a child my sensitive mind
registered her fear response whenever a dog appeared. I
learned that dogs are dangerous. Even though I'd never been
bitten and had known only one person who was bitten, my
body reacted with a fear response whenever I saw a strange
dog until I realized the origin of the fear and worked through
it.

Fear is created not by the world around us, but
in the mind, by what we think is going to happen.
                                    -Elizabeth Gawain

The good news about learned fear is that it can be *un-*
learned. It is possible for us to release ourselves from the grasp
of borrowed fears and to heal and overcome ones that are ours
alone. Unlearning fear takes a strong desire to be free, a
willingness to work to retrain ourselves, and patience. In our
era of supersonic flights, split-second computers, and fast
food, we have come to expect instant gratification. Don't
expect to be served up a fear-free life just by reading this book;
self-discovery, growth, and change do not work that way.
Yes, there will be sudden, breathtaking insights; but without
patient work and commitment to a day-to-day process of
change, they will quickly fade.

I have been working for twenty-five years to remove my tenacious fear of rejection. When I first began, patience was by no means my strong suit, and there were times when I felt discouraged to the point of despair. Sometimes I would backslide or creep forward slowly; but I can truly say that now, my fear of rejection is only a tiny thread, a fragile web limiting my life, whereas when first discovered, it was a heavy chain and anchor.

Of course fear may also be learned as a result of traumatic experiences. Many women fear men because they have been raped, molested, or otherwise physically or emotionally abused. If some frightening thing has happened to you, you will probably need the help of a minister, therapist, or other trained professional to help in uncovering and healing your inner wounds.

No matter what our past, we can relearn our fundamental attitudes toward life and also experience the deep truth that our life and relationships need not be fear-filled. We do not consist of our fear; we merely experience it. Thus we can learn step by step to see fear not as something that we *are* but something that we *have*. For example, you may have at times told yourself, I'm such a coward! Not true! Never accept a definition of yourself that identifies you as your fear. You may feel fearful, but that doesn't mean you're a coward. Any committed attempt you make to disidentify yourself from your fears deserves to be called brave, even heroic.

As you begin to disidentify with paralyzing fear, you'll start to have more control over your life. Gradually, you will learn to see yourself as larger and stronger than your fears. Moving from *re*acting to your fear to acting *on* it, allows you to be much more independent and authentic.

Here's an exercise in disidentification: The next time you're aware of feeling afraid, acknowledge what you fear, accept that it's a fact of your being at the moment, and then repeat several times to yourself: I have a fear of (heights, failure, oysters, etc.), but *I* am not this fear!

We have come to believe that we are what we feel. Not so! Feelings are absolutely important, but they aren't the totality of who we are. We are much, much more than our feelings. You might try this further exercise: Think of some sentences that appeal to you as accurate definitions of who you are. For example:

I am a pure center of self-consciousness.
I am.
I am perfectly okay as is.
I am too amazing to fathom.
I am a child of God.

Then, choose the sentence that is most powerful to you and add it to the foregoing affirmation of disidentification. I might say: I have a fear of rejection, but I am not this fear. I am a beautiful, unique soul created in God's image. Use whatever works for you. This is a powerful tool to keep you from being sucked into the vortex of your fear.

Buried Fears

We can't always be protected as we're growing up, so it's inevitable that we've had experiences that range from rather scary to completely terrifying. When something happens to us as small children, we often have no way to verbalize our feelings thereby letting others know that we need help and healing. Children who can communicate their feelings, whether through bad behavior or a good, healthy scream, are the lucky ones. Less fortunate are those children who repress frightening incidents, shutting them away from conscious awareness.

Up to approximately age seven, children often feel responsible for the events that happen in their lives. If a parent dies, or if their parents argue, the young child feels it must be his or her fault. The child's developing ego structure is not yet able to perceive cause and effect as pertaining to others. When we are children, we see ourselves as the center of the universe, the pivotal point around which all events revolve, therefore we tend to assume responsibility for whatever takes place. Thus, children who repress their fears usually end up feeling not only fearful, but bad and unworthy as well.

The story of Victoria is a good case in point. As an adult, Victoria appeared to be well adjusted and successful. She had a good education, a fulfilling job, children, and a supportive husband. She came from an apparently loving, though straightlaced and repressive family. When she entered therapy, she was suffering from continuous nightmares, a crushing fear of going to bed alone, chronically low self-esteem, and acute suicidal tendencies. She felt crazy, and the question Why? haunted her.

Victoria blamed herself for not snapping out of her depression. After losing an alarming amount of weight and thinking constantly of suicide, she sought therapy. With support from her husband and from me as her therapist, and with tremendous courage on her part, she allowed a series of long-buried memories to rise to conscious awareness.

Beginning in infancy, Victoria had been repeatedly sexually molested and physically threatened. Because her fear was so great and her sense of shame and guilt so powerful, she had repressed all conscious awareness of these atrocities. Not until she was thirty-six years old and faced with overwhelming personal crises did her defenses begin to crumble.

Painful as Victoria's memories were, it was extremely important that they emerge from hiding, from the dungeons where she'd kept them locked away. Now there was a known reason for her seemingly groundless fears. She was not crazy, as she had thought. The fears she'd experienced were entirely appropriate, considering what she had endured as a child. Now healing could begin.

Our fears are clues that there are hidden things inside of us that need healing. As you can see from the extreme example of Victoria, unresolved fears can be debilitating, even life-threatening. Having the courage to search for the source of our fears is a necessary first step toward being who we really are, free from limitations and able to live our lives to our fullest potential.

If you are experiencing fears that seem rootless, out of all proportion to the apparent cause or having no "logical" basis, give yourself a priceless gift: explore them. Only when they're brought to conscious awareness will you be able to discover how to overcome them. So long as fear remains hidden, you'll have no choice in the matter—you'll be held helplessly in its clutches.

Most hidden fears are stashed away because at one time it seemed safer to hide them than to be aware of them. When they emerge, you may experience the original fears all over again. Thus, it's essential to find a climate of safety in which to explore them. You must be able to have the conviction that the risk you're taking in exposing the origin of your fears is something you can safely handle. Before you begin to explore, find a person or group with whom you feel safe, and whom you can trust implicitly with your vulnerability.

Since the origin of our fears most often lies in childhood, we can expect to experience childlike fear while rediscovering them. Seeking emotional support at such times is not dependency; it is wisdom.

There will be many times on our road toward being ourselves that we'll need the support of others as we learn to disidentify from our fears. Wouldn't you think it self-defeating if a friend were run over by a truck but wouldn't allow doctors to set her broken bones or friends to aid her in her convalescence? Letting others nurture and support us at certain times helps us heal more quickly. When we're run over by an emotional truck, it's silly to think we shouldn't burden other people. The facade of stiff-upper-lip encourages repression, not healing. Repression imprisons; healing frees.

Fear Creates Reality

In some way, which most of us don't understand fully, fear is like a magnet that attracts to us the things we fear the most. For instance, if we fear public speaking—and it is said this is the most prevalent fear we have—and approach the podium quaking in our boots and deathly afraid we'll forget our message, it is likely we will have a lapse of memory. If our mind is tuned to an internal channel that consistently repeats fearful litanies, fear will be our experience. But we can change the channel! A helpful technique in this respect is to avoid negative statements that begin with I am:

I am fearful.
I am scared of authority.
I am unemployable.
I am a 'fraidy cat.
I am a coward.
I am ugly.

Such statements are self-fulfilling. If we wear negative name tags, we'll attract negative company. In this way our inner thoughts and feelings create our external circumstances.

Many martial-arts instructors believe that attitude is just as important as the physical movements of their particular discipline. Thus they concentrate on instilling attitudes of confidence and safety in their students. Granted, it helps to know how to defend ourselves physically from attack, but at least as important is releasing any victim feelings that we may be carrying.

Breaking out of the victim mode can be tough, and it usually helps a great deal to find a qualified instructor or therapist who can guide you. If you've been a victim of abuse, incest, rape, or some other form of violation, please seek professional help. The wounds caused by such traumatic experiences may be much deeper than you realize, and to heal them effectively requires expert guidance.

But we can all help ourselves with this simple technique. Instead of using "I am" statements when talking about your fears, say:

I have a fear of (rejection, etc.).
I sometimes experience a fear of (authority).
I can at times feel like a (coward).
I have a fear of (failure/success).
When I stand up in front of a group, I feel
    (nervous, tongue-tied, dumb).

With such statements, you acknowledge that you have fears, but you don't identify yourself as *being* a mainfestation of them. The difference is subtle, but important: You have fears, and you can heal them. You are not your fears.

As you learn to heal your fears, you'll learn also to act without letting them limit you. These days, whenever I notice a fear crying out in my body, I say: Thanks, Body, I hear you. Then I check it out to see if the fear is currently valid or an old response. If it is an old pattern, something I can do very well without now, I say to it: I'm going to go ahead and do what I need to do as if you weren't there.

Too often, a wrong interpretation of our fears prevents us from acting. We believe we shouldn't be feeling fear and so we try waiting until we feel perfectly at ease before tackling the difficulty or challenge that lies before us. This strategy never works. Many of our accomplishments happen in spite of fear. In fact, in many instances, anxiety and fear can actually propel us into action.

Bill Russell of the Boston Celtics—and one of the all-time greats of pro basketball—would get so nervous before each game that he'd vomit; yet he never let his fear keep him from being a world-class player. There's something especially heroic about his having used his talent to the utmost despite his fears.

One of my hobbies is acting. I love auditioning, and I thrive on rehearsals because creating a character is such a thrill for me. But the first night in front of an audience is agony. I am *terrified.* I wonder why I ever decided to do something so ridiculous. Why have I set myself up to fail? Surely I'll make a complete fool of myself and let the cast down in the process. All of my lines vanish from memory. In short, I have a colossal case of stage fright.

To a lesser degree, the same thing happens each time I stand up in front of a group to lead a seminar or give a talk. But I assure myself I have something worthwhile to say and do it anyway. Once I get into the swing of it, I have a great time. It's almost as if the energy generated by my fear propels me into doing a better job.

This process can backfire, as it did for me on one memorable occasion. It happened at a high-school "Lit Night" where all of the literary clubs competed in speeches, monologues, and poetry readings. I was to do a funny monologue about girdles (remember those?). The girl who went on before me forgot her lines, and my reaction was cold-sweat terror that I'd forget too. Sure enough, though I knew my lines perfectly, I had tuned my mind to a panic channel and my fearful inner dialogue resulted in an actual loss of memory.

As the preceding story demonstrates, this statement from the Bible expresses a deep truth: "Lo, the thing I feared the most has come to pass." If we fear illness, we are likely to become ill. If we fear abandonment and rejection, we will most likely experience them in our lives. Speaking for myself, when I fear rejection, I approach people guardedly, inevitably making them feel that I'm cool, or that I don't trust them; thus my very fear causes the rejection I'm trying so hard to protect myself from.

I am learning not to let fear keep me from doing what I want to do. Stage fright is no picnic—I'm not exactly crazy about perspiring down to my waistband and feeling nauseated and panicky. But I've learned through experience that when I face this fear and move through it, it diminishes and I end up enjoying the very activities that activated the fear in the first place. Taking small steps despite fear is called *desensitization*. As we persevere and *do*, in spite of fear, fear begins to lose its grip on us.

Robin, a client of mine, was afraid to drive out of town. We began to desensitize her by having her (in the safety of my office) close her eyes and imagine herself driving. When anxiety arose, we did relaxation techniques. When she could visualize herself on the street and driving away from home without anxiety, she took another small step: while sitting in the driveway in her car, she visualized herself driving out of town. When she felt able to move on to a further small step, she drove about a mile from home. With small, successful steps, she mastered her fear and now feels fine driving almost anywhere.

Many of us, unfortunately, have a lifelong legacy of fear. The task before us is to outgrow that limiting inheritance and claim our true birthright: the freedom and courage to be ourselves.

You can begin immediately to transform your fears by changing your thoughts. No matter how many times fear attacks you, keep affirming that those fears are not you and that someday you will completely overcome them. Gradually, day by day, your positive affirmations will grow in strength until they begin to push back those old barriers of fear. Remember—your fears are not you, and you are not them. You can diminish them. You can act in spite of them. You can be free.

Review your past in an atmosphere of healing gentleness and self-respect. You've already done a lot of courageous work—you've survived despite obstacles. Give yourself credit for your inborn heroism, and keep working to realize your birthright of emotional freedom.

CHAPTER 7

Underlying Assumptions And Hidden Beliefs: Things We've Swallowed Whole

The first problem for all of us,
men and women, is not to learn,
but to unlearn.

-Gloria Steinem

*O*ur deep, often unconscious, beliefs and assumptions determine whether we have the courage to be ourselves or continuously cast about outside of ourselves hoping others will define who we are. In order to free ourselves from the bonds of emotional dependence we need to explore our hidden beliefs and assumptions—how we got these hidden dragons, why we're afraid to look at them, and what we can do about them once we do find the courage to observe them.

As we grow up, we are exposed to the many attitudes, ideas, feelings, and prejudices held by our parents, families, and the society at large. We absorb and mimic what we see and feel around us. We are constantly inundated by stimuli, subliminal messages, and suggestions, many of which are detrimental to our inner growth and freedom:

"You aren't the only pebble on the beach!"
"If you can't say something nice, don't say anything at all."
"You'll never be hung for your beauty."

These statements come from the book called *Momalies: As Mother Used to Say*. We all grew up hearing similar things, which were limiting because as children we believed them.

We swallowed them whole. In my opinion, that book would be better entitled *Momma Lies*.

Why *wouldn't* we believe such statements? As young children, we learn to mistrust our inherent discernment and begin to depend on our parents, teachers, and other adults to teach us the truths about life. As we grow older, we receive further instruction:

"Women should be kept barefoot and pregnant."
"A woman's place is in the home."
"Physical beauty is essential for happiness."
(And more subtly) "Men are more valuable than women."

Although we have made great strides toward equality in the past several decades, we still have a long way to go before the actions of society—and ourselves—really match the beliefs we *think* we hold. For instance, current studies of the differences between teachers' attention to boys and girls in elementary schools show that boys receive more attention, even when the teacher herself or himself believes she or he has no prejudices. In fact, the teachers argued that they were consciously committed to giving each child the same amount and quality of attention and instruction regardless of gender. In was not until they viewed videos of themselves teaching that they realized they frequently unconsciously favored boys. If intelligent and loving people, who have dedicated themselves to the extremely important yet often thankless job of teaching, reinforce—however unconsciously—society's idea of male superiority, imagine where else we must get the same idea. No wonder we are dependent and regularly feel less than!

Erroneous messages we swallow whole as children become our own underlying assumptions and implicit beliefs, and we guide our lives accordingly by becoming emotionally dependent on other people because "they must know better than we do." Since most of these notions are hidden, we're unaware of the extent to which they rule our actions and reactions—unless we consciously ferret them out in order to transform them. *Underlying* is the operative word, as these assumptions are *under* our conscious awareness, and *lie* to us about reality. Freeing ourselves from limiting and devaluing beliefs is the key to living up to our potential and expressing our authenticity.

Our assumptions govern us much as an automatic pilot guides an airplane. For example, if we have the hidden beliefs that life is hard or sex is dirty, we will have feelings that correspond to those beliefs. Thus, beliefs hidden from conscious awareness may emerge as unconsciously motivated actions. In fact, our actions will reflect our hidden feelings.

On the occasion of Jane's engagement, her father gave her the only heart-to-heart talk they'd ever had. He thought she should be told that her mother was frigid and that the possibility existed that Jane might be as well.

Up until then Jane had enjoyed sex, though she had felt a little guilty about her pleasure. Jane had been told all her life that she was just like her mother; thus the horrible thought entered her mind that she might also be frigid. She immediately tried to hide the thought from herself, but sex soon began to be a problem for her and her new husband. Only when her underlying assumptions and fears were brought to the surface, acknowledged, and accepted did she discover that she was in fact a healthy, sensual, and sexual woman. Dad had dished out the possibility of frigidity, and she had swallowed it whole.

Our unconscious assumptions generate attitudes and actions that influence our lives in ways we may be completely unaware of. They often shape our choices of husband, career, home, friends, and lifestyle.

Mary became aware that for years she had consistently chosen men who were less intelligent than she, usually men whom she could dominate. Her relationships were often painful and caused her frustrating intellectual isolation.

Mary's father, who was mentally unbalanced, dominated her mother totally. Her mother's fear of upsetting him kept her in the role of victim. Even as a young girl, Mary was aware of her mother's rage and shame because of the imbalance in the relationship. Mary had felt her mother's pain, concluded that all relationships were one-sided, and vowed that she would never be the inferior partner. Although she had repressed this awareness, she acted it out in her adult relationships by choosing men whom she could dominate. Until she discovered the underlying beliefs that were guiding her actions, Mary hadn't considered the possibility that she might live side by side with anyone as an equal partner.

How many times have you heard women say, "I just can't do (_____) or (_____)!" Here's an example of a widely held assumption: Women aren't as good at math as men are. Studies of young children have shown that girls are naturally just as adept in math as boys are. However, as girls grow up and are subjected to subtle (and not-so-subtle) messages from teachers, parents, peers, and prejudiced literature, they believe the lie; they begin to live "down" to others' expectations.

In grade school and early high school, I received all A's in math and received the highest grade in my sophomore class on a standardized geometry test. Sometime after my sophomore year, though, I began to buy into the popular belief that girls can't do math. Much of my adult life I felt dazed by a bank statement. I thought, I can't do this. And, consequently, I couldn't.

As we uncover hidden beliefs that limit us, and replace them with valid assumptions and realizations, we take a giant step toward changing our behavior, our feelings, and our lives. By healing false assumptions and attitudes, we create whole new patterns of behavior for ourselves; we open doors toward being who we really are. Breaking out of limiting beliefs is not a selfish act, for each time we free ourselves from restrictions, we create a pattern of growth that encourages others to travel into and heal their own wounded inner regions.

Beliefs

Each of us functions within a set of beliefs. In our lives, belief systems create order and structure. They make important decisions easier, and they provide the basis for our ethics, morality, and philosophy. Our personalities are structured by the beliefs we learned from parents, teachers, friends, and the culture around us.

Our parents' beliefs have become our own. As adults we no longer need to be told right from wrong because our parents' voices are ingrained in us, telling us how to behave and what's expected of us.

Our beliefs also arise from the ways we interpret what we see and hear as we grow up. And it's interesting to note that our beliefs frequently are based far more on interpretation than on fact. Mildred always cut the end off the ham before baking it. She never questioned the logic of that behavior until her son asked her about it one day. She did it because her mother did it. When he probed further, her son discovered that his grandmother had a very logical explanation: her baking pan was too small to accommodate a whole ham. Mildred's belief was based not on an acknowledged truth but on her own, unexamined interpretation of her mother's actions as right and proper, whatever their origin.

Our belief systems can also be created from fear. If we fear rejection, we may believe that it isn't safe to disagree with others. When our views run contrary to popular opinion, we may find it hard to speak our minds. Why? Because we fear we'll be rejected.

The culture around us propagates inaccurate beliefs, too, such as: Men are more powerful than women, and Men should make more money because they have families to support. (Actually, one of every three families in America today is wholly supported by a woman.)

We give lip service to the idea that a woman's work in the home is as important as a man's work—until it comes to assigning a dollar value to the work performed. Women too easily acquiesce to the prevalent belief that the money the husband brings home is his to mete out as he sees fit. The belief that we have no money of our own can keep us feeling dependent on the men in our lives, confused about our rights, and limited in our choices. A woman who believes she is powerless to have or make money will feel unable to stop destructive behavior in the home, including physical and emotional abuse.

Although we need beliefs to guide us, false beliefs handicap us. One detrimental form of false belief is unquestioned assumptions about other women:

Women are over-emotional.
Women are catty and petty.
Women can't be trusted.
Women aren't as capable as men.

When my first husband left me for my best friend, I began to believe that women can't be trusted. Yet, with that one painful exception (and a few excruciating high-school traumas) that hadn't been my experience with women. I felt I couldn't trust them, yet my life was virtually filled with trustworthy women. My new belief created paradoxes in my

life, and since the rational mind has difficulty with paradoxes, I buried the conflict in my subconscious—thereby creating some pretty irrational feelings toward my loyal friends.
Fortunately, the origins of my distrust began to dawn on me,
and I was able to talk to my friends and free myself from the
inner turmoil.

An extremely important part of our work toward emotional growth and change will come from examining our
belief systems regarding all areas of life. Especially important
are our beliefs about other women, because negative beliefs
about our women friends will separate us from the very
people who can share and empathize with us in our triumph
over emotional dependence. All of us are in the process of
evolving from second-class citizenship. When we isolate
ourselves from other women, we are subtly isolating ourselves from ourselves.

To gain the courage to be yourself, you need to address
the beliefs that are keeping you stuck where you are. What
beliefs have you swallowed whole that you now find aren't
working for you? What beliefs, assumptions, and attitudes
are you holding onto even though they no longer enhance
your life? It is time to free yourself from worn-out, happiness-
killing beliefs such as you have to say yes to everyone, you
don't have enough talent or experience to get a great job, or
you will never have a supportive and exciting love relationship?

Seed Sentences: Weeds or Flowers?

Seed sentences are clusters of ideas, words, or scripts that
we all create in order to keep us congruent with our underlying assumptions and hidden beliefs. If our seed sentences are
self affirming and supportive, we are naturally independent,
creative, and excited about life. These are what I call flower

sentences. When they are derogatory we will very likely be emotionally dependent and find it difficult to be ourselves. These are weeds.

Most seed sentences remain unspoken, perhaps even subconscious. They are bits and pieces of ideas we've picked up along the way until they form the heart of our beliefs about ourselves. Seed sentences come from many sources—parents, TV, movies, magazines, advertising—and contribute to our ideas of how we're supposed to live and what we expect to receive from life and from others. Our lives, in effect, sprout from these seed sentences we carry within.

If all of our seed sentences blossomed into flowers, our lives would be gardens filled with beauty and grace. Unfortunately, most of us have picked up weed seeds that grow into thistles and thorns, choking our spontaneity and the realization of our authentic selves.

Some examples of flower seed sentences:

I am a worthwhile person.
I deserve to be loved.
I am lovable.
I can do anything I set my mind to.

If seed sentences such as these are germinating in your subconscious, you probably have a wonderful life, filled with loving relationships. When you look in the mirror in the morning, you are happy with what you see.

Weed sentences sound something like this:

I can never do anything right.
I don't deserve to be loved.
I'm no good at (_____) or)_____).
 Everyone handles things better than I do.

If you constantly use weed sentences, you undoubtedly feel pretty down on yourself. When people try to love you, you question their motives. How can they love *me*? They must not be very bright. Weed sentences go hand in hand with low self-esteem.

Brenda, a high-school senior, felt that she was a loser. Her seed sentences were: I'm too fat. Thunder Thighs is my name. I'm too stupid. (She had an A-minus average.) I'm not attractive to boys. I'll never find an awesome guy who will like me!

With these weed sentences buzzing in her head, she had developed a caustic exterior that scared people away. Whenever she had a crush on a boy and he ventured to look past her tough facade, she began to consider him a geek. Anyone interested in her was surely a loser. This double bind kept her from having what she wanted.

In therapy, we began to pull some of her weed sentences and replace them with lovely and more truthful flower sentences. Eventually, she went off to college leaving not one but two very nice young men sorry to see her go.

Another person who demonstrated the power of seed sentences is Connie. On the afternoon when she received her master's degree, Connie remembered her first-grade teacher saying to her mother, "It's nice that Connie is pretty, because she's not very bright." She took that to heart, and no matter how good her grades were in school, she felt dumb. Her teacher's comment had become an internalized seed sentence: I'm pretty, but I'm dumb. Quite a weed!

How do we pick up our packet of thought-seeds? People make the most unbelievably careless statements within the sensitive hearing of children: "She has a face only a mother could love." or "You're about as graceful as a bull in a china shop." Children take such pronouncements as authoritative, because they come from people who're ten feet tall.

"But I was only teasing . . ." Every hear that one? It didn't make you feel any better, did it? Teasing is veiled hostility and is almost never funny, unless the teasee has openly agreed to relate that way. There is gentle, loving teasing, but in my estimation, about ninety-eight percent of the time teasing is hurtful.

No matter how old we are, we all have sensitive areas through which insidious sentences can penetrate to our subconscious minds. We are all especially vulnerable to certain types of suggestion. For example, I once discovered a seed sentence I'd been carrying around since childhood: Women are not happy. No one had told me that, but as a little girl I *felt* it was true. The women I knew didn't seem very happy: they sighed and complained, and to me that meant unhappiness. As I grew up, I collected data that supported my underlying belief that women weren't happy. One of my mother's favorite laments, uttered with a sigh or from between clenched teeth, was: A man may work from sun to sun, but a woman's work is never done. I asked myself, How can women be happy if they have to work all the time? Another weed seed for unhappiness.

Perhaps predictably, my first marriage was unhappy, and only gradually did I realize that my unhappiness had preceded my marriage. Strange as it may sound, I was uncomfortable when I felt happy. Whenever I felt myself becoming happy, I'd get scared because I felt somehow off balance, so I'd pick a fight, become moody, or sabotage a pleasant situation. Unhappiness was my unconscious comfort zone. Being unhappy kept me congruent with my underlying belief that women were not happy.

When I began to be aware of my self-defeating underlying belief, I started to work on changing it. Bit by bit, I gave myself permission to be happy. Every time I spotted the old pattern of happiness-sabotage, I stopped and reassured myself that it was okay to feel this good. I replaced my weed sentences with: I have the right to be happy; It is okay to feel great! I'm now very comfortable with happiness, and I've invented some new seed sentences to affirm this new awareness: Women deserve to be happy *and* have fun!; *I* deserve to be happy and have fun!

We gravitate toward the familiar and shun the unknown. When we go against our seed sentences, we feel a loss of integrity with ourselves. We don't trust what is outside of our experience. My experience had been that the women I knew weren't happy. That doesn't mean it was necessarily true of the grown-ups I observed, only that I perceived it to be true. Pulling the negative weed sentence from my subconscious has helped me to be who I really am—a fundamentally happy woman.

In the midst of a pleasant afternoon with her brother and his family, Lily found herself becoming depressed for no apparent reason. As she traced the thread of her thoughts, she discovered a seed sentence working in the background: All good things must come to an end. She had begun to grieve over her relatives' departure hours before the time had come. Her seed sentence was conditioning her to be wary of loss. She couldn't enjoy the moment because of its foreshadowed ending.

Pulling our emotional weeds is important because internalized seed sentences such as, "If I'm rejected, I'll die" sound dramatic and grandiose; but the internal not-okay child in us actually perceives rejection as life-threatening. When we become aware of such debilitating seed sentences, we can start the process of replacing them with opposite, healing thoughts. With our new awareness of the inner terror of life-threatening rejection, we are free to choose thoughts that help us become consciously self-directed rather than unconsciously controlled. Becoming aware of our crippling and fear-provoking weed sentences and replacing them with liberating and affirming flower sentences leads us to the emotional independence of making our own decisions based on what is right for us rather than on what we fear. And that's what emotional independence is all about.

Two of the most powerful forces that shape our beliefs are religion and society. Often, I think they deserve to be known as The Brothers Grim. In the past, women have rarely questioned the truth or reality of religious and societal assumptions. And they've felt powerless to change what they felt was erroneous. Feeling helpless sinks us more deeply into emotional dependence.

One of our greatest foes has been our own internal sense of authority, which has kept us believing whatever our political, cultural, and religious institutions have told us about women. Until just a few years ago, men virtually owned "their" women. As soon as she married, a woman's property became her husband's. (This is still the case in many countries.) Fathers paid new husbands dowries to assume responsibility for their daughters. This may have made certain women feel materially secure, but it hardly encouraged young women to think of themselves as unique and valuable.

Have you ever secretly believed that society felt sorry for your father because you weren't a boy? Worse, have you ever thought your parents were disappointed because you were a girl? Many of us have picked up our society's passed-down belief that women are in various respects "less than" men.

While many of us can look back at our early religious affiliations and feel that they gave us security, love, and the encouragement to become our best selves, others aren't so fortunate. What we heard in church was: "Lord, forgive me a miserable sinner." In many organized religions, guilt and sin are bedrock concepts. All men (!) were born sinners, and if you sin you'll suffer anything from eternal roasting in a molten lake of fire to many lifetimes of atonement for the bad karma you've incurred.

The word "sin" is actually a archery term which means "to miss the mark"—a far more kindly interpretation than it's given by many orthodox religions. In fact, few denominations are satisfied with the Bible's definitions of sin (in the Ten Commandments, for example). Religious leaders often feel duty bound to create new sins: Not long ago a woman who showed her ankles was a Jezebel. A girl who smoked was a scarlet woman.

It pays to sort through the seed sentences you've carried over from your associations with religion and society. A remarkable number of my clients come from backgrounds of guilt-fostering religious environments. Guilt and fear keep them emotionally dependent and prevent them from experiencing their authentic selves.

Lynn is a successful businesswoman, a single mother, respected and loved in her community. She spent her childhood in a strict, church-run school where obeying the rules was the paramount requirement. She never disobeyed, but she also never felt okay about for herself, no matter how much outward approval she won. In therapy she had a vivid, painful recollection of a severe teacher telling her, "You never get it right!" Lynn, a sensitive child, internalized that thought until it became one of her basic beliefs about herself, accompanied by the seed sentence: I never do it right. As an adult, even though she more often than not *did* do it right, she never *felt* like a person who did things correctly.

Spirituality is probably the most important aspect of ourselves that we humans need to explore and expand, but I don't think we can experience our authentic spiritual selves until we have ferreted out the unquestioned, self-condemning beliefs we've acquired in our contact with society and some orthodox religions.

Many of our semiconscious seed sentences express fear

of offending others. The trouble is, our freedom diminishes if we are afraid of standing up to others. I don't mean that I advocate unkindness or discourtesy—it's very important for our own self-esteem to think empathetically of others. But craving others' approval in order to feel okay about ourselves kills creativity and authenticity.

Women have a tendency to shackle themselves to others' moods. What happens when your husband, boss, or kids are in a lousy mood and nothing pleases them? Do you dance around like a trained bear, trying to make them laugh and be happy? I used to do that, because I always felt that I was somehow to blame for other people's bad moods. When they were rejecting, I felt I was less of a person. Their rejection was unbearable, and so I tried to dance to whatever tune they were inaudibly playing. It never worked, and I became increasingly angry with myself for behaving like a doormat.

In freeing myself from emotional dependence, I've learned that, to paraphrase the words of an excellent book by Laura Huxley, "I am not the target." I've learned how to step back from the situation. In the presence of angry or rejecting vibrations my stomach still knots up, my throat closes, and I want to run to the nearest cookie jar for solace, but I say to my body and my internal little girl: We're okay! We're safe! With reassurance from these powerful new seed sentences, I find my fright dissipating, and end up feeling very pleased with myself. A threatening situation is transformed into a pleasant inner victory; another bout of fear is positively overcome without my falling into the dependence trap.

The following is a list of common weed sentences and nicknames. What seed sentences did you gather as you grew up? List them in the space provided. Look at your seed sentences and begin to negate their power with your awareness. As you replace weed sentences with flowers, you'll be freed from their stranglehold on your behavior. Are your seed sentences roses, lilies, and jonquils? or pyracantha, poison ivy, and stinkweed?

You can pull up your weed thoughts and replace them with thought flowers that will blossom into a beautiful life.

Weed Sentences:
Things We've Swallowed Whole

1. I should have been a boy.
2. Tears are a form of self-pity.
3. Wear a girdle and keep your legs crossed . . . nice girls don't . . .
4. Nice girls do more than their share.
5. Women are not happy.
6. I am responsible for another person's happiness.
7. Women/men can't be trusted.
8. It's a cruel world out there.
9. Women over forty aren't attractive.
10. I'm ugly, unlovable, (_____) or (_____).
11. I can't . . .
12. Don't air your dirty laundry in public.
13. I've always got to be "up."
14. Nothing I do is good enough.
15. That's men's work (or that's women's work).
16. The children are totally my responsibility.
17. My sister (lover, brother, father, dog) is better than I am.
18. Life is hard and then you die.

Your Own Weed Sentences

1._____

2._____

3._____

4._____

5._____

6._____

Nicknames

1. Chubby Cheeks
2. Lardo
3. Fatty Patty
4. Stick
5. Freck (as in freckles)
6. Sappy Sue
7. Four Eyes
8. Thunder Thighs
9. Bucky
10. Baby
11. Rug Rat
12. Schnoz

Some of Your Nicknames

1._____

2._____

3._____

4._____

Freeing ourselves from underlying assumptions and working to bring our beliefs into harmony with the goal of loving support for ourselves takes time and doesn't come easily. We need to be gentle with ourselves and remember that we are called upon to love our neighbors *as* ourselves, not to the exclusion of ourselves. As a natural outgrowth of loving ourselves, we will learn to love others more fully and authentically.

Become aware of your beliefs. Bring them into the light of your present, adult knowledge. Gently acknowledge that they are what they are. Then accept that they constitute what you've believed until now, and that you can transform them into beliefs that allow you to fully express who you really are. Finally, begin working patiently to change them.

CHAPTER 8

Women's Faces of Fear

Fear is a question. What are you afraid of, and why? Our fears are a treasure house of self-knowledge if we explore them.

-Marilyn Ferguson

*B*ecause we women become so conditioned by our fears, we spend much of our life reacting automatically rather than *acting* creatively and appropriately. The tyranny of unexplored fear keeps us tied to outmoded patterns of emotionally dependent behavior. If we don't consciously face our internal dragons of fear, they have the nasty habit of emerging from their caves in destructive forms. I call these unconscious and painful behavior motifs the Faces of Fear.

Fear wears many faces, and we each have fears that are unique to us—fears that result in negative feelings or behaviors. I've chosen to discuss six ways we disguise fear that I have found to be almost universal among the women with whom I work. Exploring these common faces of fear—and how we act as a result of them—gives us a model for transforming fear into positive and growth-producing energy. Fear *can* act as an impetus rather than an impediment.

Appeasing
Fatigue
Resistance
Addiction
Illness
Depression

Appeasing

Dictionary definitions of *appease* include, "to pacify; give in to the demand, either silent or spoken, of another." My own definition is, "to try to make 'it' okay for the other guy, to take responsibility for his or her life, to placate at the expense of yourself and your feelings of worth." Sounds a lot like co-dependence and emotional dependence, doesn't it? Feels like it too!

For many women, appeasing is a familiar pattern. How often do we appease the man in our lives by giving in to his moods and desires, even if it doesn't feel right for us? Or acquiesce to our children's demands when we really don't believe they're reasonable?

Our need for connection is one of the main reasons we are so prone to appeasing behavior. It seems this need is inherent, or socially conditioned early on—no one knows for sure--far more in girls than in boys. As described in *In a Different Voice*, Harvard University researcher Carol Gilligan studied pre-school children and found that even at that early age, girls were much more appeasing than boys. Girls wouldn't disagree over the rules of a game but would try to make peace in order to preserve the relationships among their playmates. When arguments erupted boys needed to honor the rules of the game and would sacrifice closeness with their peers in order to maintain their stance. Gilligan concluded that girls more than boys, for whatever reasons, value emotional connectedness.

As adults, women seem to cultivate their need for emotional connectedness. We give ourselves away constantly in order to feel connected to others; it's as if we feared "death by disconnection."

We try to appease people because we fear rejection, disapproval, and separation. Confrontation scares us: we feel uncomfortable when we disagree. Our stomachs churn and our throats tighten with fear. We're afraid that "they" may disagree with us, disapprove of us, dislike us, reject us, or even leave us. We dread feeling emotionally separated and abandoned.

Early in our lives, we women learn to "make nice" in order to appease those with whom we want to stay connected. When we were children, our parents' disapproval felt life-threatening. As we grew older, we transferred our emotional, and sometimes economic, dependence from parents to peers, boyfriends, mates, and government agencies.

Although women are making great strides toward economic independence, financial dependence remains a reality that often keeps us in unhappy and unhealthy situations. Even if we are independently wealthy, emotionally it still feels life-threatening to be out of favor with our mates, children, co-workers, or friends. Through fear of emotional isolation, we too easily give up our independence.

Not only do women have a need for closeness, we've been trained by society to be peacemakers. Many of us consider it our job to be the emotional lighthouse for those around us. Whenever someone seems to be in danger of hitting the rocks emotionally, we feel it's our duty to jump in and rescue them. We appease in order to purchase peace at any price.

Do you sacrifice your independence in order to keep the peace in your family or at work? If so, do you find yourself, inwardly seething and feeling resentful and ripped-off? If you do, the price you are paying is lack of inner peace, and low self-esteem. Quite a concession!

Appeasing is one of the ways we give ourselves away. Women often say in response to their own feelings, needs, wants, or to a hurtful remark made carelessly, "Oh, well, I'll let that go. It's not worth the effort to deal with it." What you're really saying is, *I'm* not worth the effort. We are the only caretakers of our feelings of worth. Consciously or unconsciously we teach people how to treat us! It's uncanny how, when we don't feel worthy, those around us see us as unworthy and begin to use us as emotional dishrags to clean up all their messes. This kind of emotional dependence is excruciating. I know, because I used to be a chronic appeaser.

I was terrified of rejection. In my deep inner self, in the scared little girl I carried with me, I feared I would die if I were rejected. So I avoided confrontation. I remember a time when a friend hurt my feelings through a joking remark made in the company of others. I was crushed because she had jabbed one of my most vulnerable areas, but I smiled to cover my hurt and let the remark go. I even felt a little guilty for being hurt and angry as if, somehow, I deserved the put-down. Thankfully, that would not happen now! Through therapy, and through honest talks with myself and with friends, I learned to love and comfort my inner child whenever she felt rejected. Now I let her know she won't die, because she can always count on *me* to be there for her emotionally. With my inner child protected, I am free to clear any misunderstandings or hurts between myself and others.

I often see appeasing behavior in other women, especially in relation to their mates. I recently watched a friend try repeatedly to mollify her husband. She had wanted to go to a concert, and he agreed to go with her. During the performance, she kept checking with him to see if he was enjoying it. If she sensed that he was disgruntled, she would rub his back and talk cajolingly to him as if to say, Please, please enjoy yourself, so that I can enjoy myself. Later, she became aware of the fear that had prompted her behavior. Whenever her husband disapproves, he withdraws into icy moodiness. She felt that if he were bored, he would disapprove of her for having suggested they go. Her life with him is a vicious circle: the fear of feeling rejected causes her to appease him, which

104

in turn makes her mad at herself and at him.

Appeasing behavior is the negative face of a very power-ful gift that women can offer to the world, that of nurturing people and making intimate connections with them. I've learned not to appease, but I *do* compromise. Appeasing behavior comes from a fearful, powerless place inside of us, a place where there is very little choice. On the other hand, conscious compromise comes from our adult, empowered self, the part of us that knows we have the ability to *choose*. If we are to be in relationships with others, there will always be times when compromising is appropriate; but we need to do so from a center of inner honesty and integrity—a place of strength and flexibility. That's a far cry from giving yourself away.

What to do About Appeasing Behavior

Appeasing isn't an easy habit to break. The first step is to become aware of yourself as you do it. When you think about this, try to be very specific. Exactly how do you appease? And whom do you appease? Is it your husband, children, mother, or father-in-law? When you become aware of appeasing behavior, stop and pay attention to how you feel. Like every-one else who appeases, you'll probably discover that you feel resentful, angry, and embarrassed.

Once you've become aware of your appeasing behavior, you can choose to act in a different way. The old yearning to appease will still be present, but as you continue to act in a respectful and authentic way toward yourself and others, the need to appease will gradually dissipate.

The trick to changing appeasing behavior is to increase your tolerance for emotional separation. When you can learn to say to yourself, *Oh well, I see we'll be separate for a little while now. How can I take care of myself in that time?*, then you'll have begun to break the chain that binds you to appeasing behavior.

As I was changing my need to appease, it was important for me to put some distance between myself and the persons from whom I felt emotionally separated. When I stayed in close proximity to them, the urge to overcome my pain by appeasing behavior was almost overwhelming. So I took care of myself by getting out of the house.

What can you do when you feel rejected and need to strengthen your sense of self-worth? Call a friend. Go to a movie. Commune with nature. Write in your journal. Talk to and take care of your inner child. Face your fears squarely, and then choose to stop the automatic, destructive behaviors they usually evoke. You will not die. You will survive.

Acknowledge your feelings to the person or persons involved. If that isn't possible, or if it wouldn't be constructive, tell your feelings to a friend or to a therapist—even to your dog or cat, if necessary—or express them in a private journal. Accept the fact that you've been an appeaser, and that you can choose to behave differently now.

Periods of change are full of paradoxes. They're difficult but exciting, frightening but freeing. Letting go of old patterns that no longer work for us is exhilarating. As we learn to replace appeasing behavior with assertive, self-valuing patterns, we begin to feel mature and equal in our relationships. Study the fears that keep you appeasing: look at them, examine them, bring them out into the open. As you learn about them, and consciously adopt positive counter-behaviors, your fears will dissipate, and you'll break out of the cycle of appeasement.

Fatigue

Are you and your women friends always tired? One of the

quickest ways to become exhausted is by suppressing your feelings—burying them in the dungeon of your subconscious. This process has been called "gunnysacking": anything we don't want to see or experience, we stuff into an emotional gunnysack; and as we hide more and more feelings, the sack gets bigger and heavier. Carrying around an oppressive bag full of unresolved and unspoken feelings leaves us so fearful and drained that we have no energy to stand up for ourselves or be independent.

If you are a sack toter it's no small wonder you feel fatigued—it's very tiring to lug around a bag of fears, hurts, and disappointments, holding tight to the drawstring so they won't sneak out and overwhelm you. It's like sitting on a trapdoor through which many rebellious gremlins are trying to rise.

If chronic fatigue is an issue in your life, it may be that you're harboring feelings that need to be looked at and moved through. It's much harder work for our minds and bodies to avoid the feelings that need attention—to stuff them down, ignore them, or put off dealing with them—than it is to face them. It takes an enormous amount of energy to hide from ourselves and others the dark feelings and thoughts we *all* have.

We say to ourselves, Maybe if I ignore it, it'll go away. But of course it doesn't. Our unacknowledged feelings merely grow bigger, more ruthless and uncontrollable. In the long run, facing feelings is less work and infinitely more rewarding.

Often, fatigue is a signal from our wise body and mind alerting us to hidden feelings. If you feel too threatened by your buried feelings to uncover them alone, seek professional guidance. Your fatigue is telling you it's time to lighten the inner load.

Resistance

It's human nature to resist what we fear. This face of fear, resistance, is quite clever: whenever we're challenged to change, it hides behind righteous indignation at how unfair and unfeeling people and circumstances are.

Some people resist everything—from the weather, fate, and aging to ball scores, their spouses, and politics. We think of such people as negative and grumpy; in reality, they're afraid. They fear everything that involves risk, change, or loss of control. Rather than look within themselves and change their own reactions, they blame the world outside.

Resistance loves to put on disguises:

"I forgot..."
"They didn't call me."
"I overslept."
"I'm too tired."
"It doesn't matter anyway."
"Why change? It's okay the way it is."
"It's too hard."
"I could never do that!"
"You shouldn't feel that way."
"That's dumb!"
"Isn't it awful?"
"I'm too fat (or too old) for that!"
"I can't."
"Why is it always me who has to change?"

The best way to overcome resistance is to gently push on it. When you notice yourself becoming negative, laugh about it if you can. Magnify your gripes until they become ridiculous. The more lightly you deal with your resistance, the easier it'll be to move through it. Look at your resistance and, from the wiser, lighter part of your mind, choose to act anyway.

When I began to write this book, I came face-to-face with gigantic obstacles of resistance. After all, what did I have to say that would be worthwhile to anybody? They might laugh at my efforts. And just think of the sheer work involved!

My insecure inner self stepped forward sneeringly when I lost my tape recorder and the notes of my first meeting with my literary publicist. (I'd put them on top of the car and they scattered all over the road as I drove away.) I realized then that I was anxious about writing the book—*terrified* is a better word—and I spoke about it aloud. I honored the fear and didn't act on it. I stopped resisting the long process of writing the book, and promised myself I would take it one small step at a time. Working through my initial resistance was essential; if I hadn't dealt with it, I would never have completed the book.

Sharon, a client of mine, told me, "I've been really bothered by something you said last week." I had told her to gently look at any resistance she had toward therapy. She was convinced she wasn't resisting. She said she loved our time together; and yet, she was ten minutes late to her first session, and twenty minutes late to the second because her "husband wouldn't hurry." She missed the third session altogether, and was late again to the fourth.

As we talked about her behavior, she agreed that, yes, it was scary to come to therapy and she feared what she might find out about herself. Consciously, she was eager to learn and grow; subconsciously, she was frightened. As soon as she became aware of her resistance, she no longer needed to be late. She acknowledged her fear to herself and to me, and we both accept it whenever it arises. She is learning to let it go, piece by piece.

Resistance keeps us stuck in a narrow range of behaviors,

thoughts, and feelings. Whenever we begin to push the boundaries of our safe range, resistance plants itself firmly in our path. Going outside our comfort zone activates hidden fears of the unknown.

Resistance is a twisted expression of a natural tendency. After all, there are many situations in which we really must protect ourselves. To strip away our healthy sense of caution suddenly and entirely would be like pulling off a protective scab. Therefore, as you begin to work on your inner resistance, do so gently, patiently, and with love.

Addiction

Over the last several years people in general have become increasingly aware of our society's tendency toward addictions of all kinds—over-eating, alcohol, drugs (prescription, over-the- counter, and illegal), and over-working, to name a few. The list could go on almost indefinitely.

If we are hiding our fears in addiction of some kind, our first reaction will probably be, *I'm* not addicted to _____! One of the major symptoms of addiction is denial. Has this so-called nonexistent problem ever evoked concerned remarks from family and friends? If so, we need to pay close attention to what it is we're trying to deny.

Hiding our fears behind a compulsive behavior of any kind severely limits our ability to be ourselves. If addiction is a problem for you, there is help around every corner—you have only to find the courage to reach out and ask. Scores of groups such as Alcoholics Anonymous, Al-Anon, Narcanon, and Over-eaters Anonymous meet daily in almost every city and town. If you feel more comfortable working on your own, bookstores are teeming with excellent recovery books. Do yourself a life-saving favor and find the help you need.

Besides being addicted to chemicals, many of us have

become addicted to chaos and calamity. Why? Because if we are swept up in a torrent of activities or traumas, it takes all of our energy just to stay afloat and we don't have to realize that our lives are not our own. We have neither the time nor the energy to say, "Is this all there is to life?" The addiction to busyness is a very effective avoidance technique. In the turmoil of overcommitment we can avoid uncomfortable issues, at least for awhile.

We aren't to blame for our fears, but it is up to us to decide how we'll handle them. We are responsible for choosing ways that lead us toward making the most of this gift of life. Our main job is to realize who and what we are and express our beauty in the world. We can't do that if we are deadened by addictions.

Illness

Repressed feelings tend to lodge in the body in the form of hidden tensions, unhealthy habits, and stress-induced chemical changes. Often, illness is an *expression* of feelings *re-pressed.*

Carl and Stephanie Simonton of the Simonton Cancer Clinic in Texas found that when terminally ill patients expressed their gunnysacked feelings of guilt, rage, fear, etc., their cancer frequently went into remission, or at least their symptoms became less acute. Dr. Bernie Siegel, a surgeon who uses love as often as a scalpel, encourages his patients to verbalize explicitly all of their feelings. An amazing number of Dr. Siegel's "terminal" patients get well.

Our bodies try to communicate with us, but all too often we don't pay attention to the signals they send. When we ignore it, our body grabs our attention in creative ways. Marge's story is a perfect example. She was going through an extremely stressful family situation and felt depleted by the emotional strain. Through fatigue and increased muscle tension, her body told her to take time to rest and replenish her energies. She ignored its message and buried herself in work and commitments, pushing herself to exhaustion.

She began to lose weight dramatically. All of her clothes hung on her and her co-workers were forever presenting their "Twiggy" with bagels and donuts, but she didn't have time to eat. One day she fainted in the post office and woke up to find herself surrounded by the concerned faces of paramedics and post-office patrons. Being a very private person, she was mortified. As Marge was being whisked away to the hospital, she made a commitment to begin listening to her body. It turned out to be a life-saving commitment because not long after her fainting spell, she found a lump in her breast and immediately had it checked. Though the tumor was malignant, she had discovered it early enough to save both her breast and her life.

Illness is a great way to resist—it seems so socially acceptable and might even get us some sympathy. Whenever Wyn and her husband fight, she gets flu symptoms. She fears confrontation not only with him but also with her own feelings. By getting sick she avoids further confrontation. Her unexplored feelings come out in the form of physical symptoms. Unfortunately, her inability to face her fears creates a lose-lose situation for herself and her husband. It spares her the discomfort of confrontation but leaves them both frustrated, angry, and confused. She's left with physical symptoms, and unresolved issues in her marriage, and she remains the uncomfortable target of his anger and frustration.

Our bodies forewarn us. Several years ago, I was sick for ten days straight—and I'm rarely sick. I had ignored many clear warning signs, and finally my overworked body said, "Okay, Sue, you asked for it," and it just quit. I *couldn't* go on. For four or five days, all I could do was rest. Even reading was too strenuous. Later, I began to think, Why did I need this illness? It became obvious to me that I'd been feeling responsible for the lives of everyone around me. I'd convinced myself that my clients couldn't make it without me, and that my family needed my constant support, ever-wise counsel, and ready sense of humor. I was indispensable!

Besides being an expression of a genuine desire to help my friends and family, my compulsion was an ego trip. I pushed and pushed—Wonder Woman flies again! But Wonder Woman finally fell into her bed and stayed there. Surprise! Everyone to whom I'd felt indispensable got along just fine. Clients survived, my professional life came back to normal very quickly, the family marched right along, friends took care of their own lives, organizations found other volunteers, and my body got its much-needed rest. Pattern broken!

The fear that led me to get sick was that if I didn't give my all, always, I wouldn't be good enough; and if I weren't good enough, surely I would be unloved and abandoned. Clients would leave, children would feel neglected, husband would be disappointed—oh, horrors! I wouldn't be *perfect!* It took illness to show me that I'd reverted to two old patterns familiar to many women: (1) taking care of everyone else first; and (2) being perfect in order to be okay.

An essential part of a happy, healthy life is being of service to others; but *indispensable is destructive.* Pace yourself in your work and commitments. Nobody is indispensable. Wonder Woman, hang up your magic bracelets! And when you get sick, honor your body; give it the rest and medical attention that it's asking for.

Not all illness is emotionally induced. A therapist friend of mine who was used to self-evaluation developed a severe headache during her aerobics class. She asked herself all the usual questions: Why do I need this? What am I not looking at? What do I need to learn from this headache? No answers came. Was she hiding something from herself? Almost as an afterthought she loosened her headband. That worked!

Be gentle with yourself. If you discover that you're using illness as an escape, or pushing yourself until you get sick, learn to change that behavior. Honor your body; if it gives out because it needs a rest, relax and enjoy it.

Depression

Depression is the classic disease of women. Why? Change two letters and instead of *de*pression you have *ex*pression. If we don't express what we're feeling—what's bugging us—in a constructive, healing manner, very often the result is depression: the way women weep without tears.

Depression is like a fog that settles over us, limiting our ability to see what we're really feeling. Often when we're depressed there's something we need to do about some situation, and we're afraid to do it.

Some kinds of depression are normal. When we experience a loss, a setback, or a shattered dream, it would be unnatural not to feel a bit depressed. Depression is one of the five normal stages of grieving as described by Dr. Elisabeth Kubler-Ross in her book, *On Death and Dying*. But most depression, and certainly chronic depression (unless due to some chemical imbalance), is a sign that we're hiding from something or avoiding action. Often, that "something" is anger.

In the psychology trade, there's an old cliche: Depression is inverted anger. That's more or less true, but depression can also be inverted anything else. I don't know about you, but when I was growing up it was not okay for me to express anger. In our family, we denied that anger existed. I felt it, in myself and coming from my parents and sister, but we did not acknowledge it. We kept it locked in a closet, where it got bigger and bigger.

I remember giving in to anger once as a teenager and swore within hearing distance of my mother. Looking back, I feel it was reasonable anger and worthy of a good shout and a swear word or two. But the punishment for expressing my anger in that way was my being forbidden to attend a dance that I had looked forward to. Also, Mother didn't speak to me for the rest of the day. So I learned to invert my anger to avoid rejection and punishment.

In order to save ourselves from the purgatory of disconnection we often resorted to emotional dependence and learned that:

*Nice girls **don't** talk that way!*
*Nice girls **don't** act aggressive.*
*Nice girls **don't** rebel.*
*Nice girls **don't** get angry at people they love.*
*Nice girls **do** learn to play the victimized, poor-me role.*
*Nice girls **do** learn to express their anger covertly,*
  in manipulative ways.
*Nice girls **do** get depressed.*
*Nice girls **do** feel paralyzed by all their repressed*
  feelings and their guilt about having such
  feelings in the first place.

If you are depressed, check and see if, down deeper, what you're really feeling is anger. Anger is natural—it's how you tell yourself, Whoa, something isn't right here! In our culture, anger and depression are labeled "bad." We believe a normal person must always be upbeat and happy.

We are only really depressed when we're not aware of our feelings. If we are aware of them and working them out, even if they are sad, we are in the very healthy process of healing.

There's a crucial point here. Don't label yourself or allow others to label you as depressed if you are in fact experiencing your authentic feelings at the moment. I'm not talking about wallowing in self-pity—that's self-defeating. I am talking about taking out your fears and angers and looking at them. That's *not* depression.

If you feel depressed, get specific: What are you feeling? Name it. Bring the dragon out into the light.

Sondra was depressed and didn't know why. With gentle exploration, we uncovered her real feeling: sadness. She was sad over the realities of a marriage in which her husband wasn't able to understand many of her feelings and needs. She felt alone, frustrated, and unhealthy. She had covered her sadness and loneliness with vague depression because she feared that voicing her real feelings would lead to her leaving him.

As a result of our working together in therapy, she discovered what she wasn't getting out of the marriage and set about finding ways to fill those needs for herself. She chose to stay in the marriage and concentrate on its many good aspects. She gave up her frustrated dependence on her husband, her expectation that he would fill all her needs; instead, she learned to work a computer, opened her own business, began to cultivate new relationships, and reconnected with friends she'd lost track of. Sondra's depression was a valuable clue that she was covering up important feelings and thereby limiting her life out of fear.

As we begin to explore our depression for underlying feelings of anger, it's very important to remember that it is hard for people to be on the receiving end of the full force of someone else's wrath. That's one reason why it's crucial we learn to stop inverting our anger, holding it in until it comes out in self-destructive depression or in an uncontrolled volcanic explosion. Slugging your mate or kicking the dog is not constructive, but it *is* constructive to punch a punching bag, knead some bread, or play an aggressive game of racquetball.

We need to accept our anger, fear, or whatever undisclosed feelings we have, no matter how socially unacceptable they seem. We are human; therefore, we will have the entire gamut of human feelings whether we think they are permissible or not. In a climate of acceptance we can learn to express our feelings in healthy and productive ways. As we expand our love and support for ourselves, the faces of fear will gradually drop away.

CHAPTER 9

Drowning in Life's Debris

Loneliness and the feeling of being unwanted is the most terrible poverty.

-Mother Teresa

*N*one of us is completely free of inner debris. We've all grieved. We all carry around unresolved emotional junk. We've all suppressed anger, guilt, and resentment. We're human, and these experiences help us to grow. But we can only grow and be who we really are by healing our inner hurts, sharing our pain, and forgiving ourselves and others. If we leave piles of unresolved emotional debris under the rug, there's always the danger that we may stumble over them and fall right into the crater of emotional dependence.

It's true that growth involves risk; but if you increase your ability to tolerate pain, you'll be able to risk acting even when you're afraid—which means that you will be in the process of breaking free from emotional dependence. As you clean the debris out from under your carpet, you'll feel an increasing sense of self-worth and independence. Not immediately, perhaps, because it takes time for the healing process to gain force and momentum. But if you work at it consistently and with patience, your healing will begin and your creativity and sense of freedom will start to flow.

Guilt

One of the biggest mounds swept under our emotional carpet is guilt. Among women, guilt spreads with the rampant fury of bubonic plague. We feel guilty if our kids don't turn out as we think they should, as our parents think they should, or as society thinks they should. I know a woman whose son was an all-around superstar in high school. In college, he burned out and left school. He didn't work much, and when he did, it was always in menial jobs. Her cry: Where did I go wrong?

Women Feel Guilty If They:

Do	*Don't*
Work	Work
Discipline the children	Discipline the children
Make more money than their husbands or fathers	Bring in "their share"
Take time for personal interests	Take time for personal interests
Get divorced	Have a happy marriage
Want free time and/or solitude	Nurture the spiritual side of their nature
Chat on the phone	Keep their friendships up
Say no	Say no
Have sex or want it	Have sex or want it
Get sick	Keep their bodies youthful and fit
Get angry	Stand up for themselves
Have children	Have children

Do you see yourself on that list? I do! I used to feel guilty if the cat had matted fur. Who said it was my responsibility to de-mat the cat? I did!

We've been led to believe that we're responsible for others' happiness, success, moods, arguments, and failures. When our families aren't happy, it's *our* fault.

According to Lynne Caine, author of *What Did I Do Wrong? Mothers, Children, Guilt*, Sigmund Freud helped perpetuate this belief. In an interview, she said:

"Our society is saturated with mother-blaming. This began, I believe, in the 1940s. That's when the popularizers of Freudian psychology discovered mothers were to blame for everything that went wrong with the American family. In 1942 Philip Wylie wrote *Generation of Vipers*, in which he proclaimed that Mom was a jerk. He coined the term 'momism.' From then on it's been open season on mothers. Mother-blaming—and in some cases mother-hating—abounds in our literature, movies, and TV. Mothers are portrayed as being either manipulative, possessive, controlling and bitchy, or as being wimpy, ineffectual and ludicrous."

This idea has become part of our belief system. For most of us, it's an underlying assumption—something we've swallowed whole. We create "Momist" seed sentences, such as: If my child, husband, or friend isn't happy, it's my fault. I need to fix my husband's life. I'm responsible for my child's successes in college.

Exaggerated affirmations of responsibility like these are loaded with guilt-producing power that keep us emotionally beholden to those who, in truth, are responsible for and to themselves. In fact, we can never *make* people happy or successful; by feeling that we must make people happy, we merely set ourselves up for inevitable disappointment.

Years ago, my husband and I took a magazine quiz to see

if we were compatible. One of the questions was: "When you and your spouse argue, is it sometimes/usually/always his/her fault?" My answer was "sometimes," and his was "always." He believed the myth that I was responsible for his happiness. Arguing made him unhappy, therefore if we argued, it must be my fault.

When we assume responsibility for another person's happiness, we set ourselves up to fail. I call it being a responsibility sponge. We become everybody's designated garbage can, with a sign on us that tells our mates, children, parents, and employers: "Dump here."

There was a time when, if there was a puddle of unhappiness around one of my kids or my husband, I was quick to leap in and try to mop it up. Having had two husbands and four kids, my sponge became extremely soggy! I believed that somehow I had failed them or offended them if they were unhappy, that it was part of my job as wife, mother, and human being never to offend anybody. But then I discovered that *our freedom diminishes if we are afraid of standing up to others.*

I truly believed it was my role to carry everyone's garbage and mop up all their puddles. If I didn't, I felt guilty. If I did and they didn't "get happy," I felt guilty and resentful. The role of responsibility sponge carries with it the need to teach others what they don't know, especially about feelings. As a therapist, I was definitely subject to that delusion. I knew all about feelings. But my husband hated my preaching; it felt to him like I was playing the combined roles of mother and teacher. Plays havoc with your love life!

While we do need loving relationships, we never need to turn our lives over to someone else, or take over responsibility for another person's life. By putting our happiness in others' hands, we become dependent; by taking responsibility for others' happiness, we invite them to become dependent—an invitation that the truly healthy human spirit always vigorously refuses.

Guilt is either appropriate or inappropriate. Appropriate guilt is a compass that tells you when you're going in the wrong direction. Like a road sign, it looms ahead, saying, "Stop. Wrong way." It's there to help; acknowledge it, and it subsides, its job done. For instance, if you make a thoughtless or hurtful remark, a twinge of guilt can be an indicator that you need to apologize.

Naturally, there's also appropriate guilt that's deep, long-lasting, and painful. That kind of intensive, appropriate guilt signals a severe deviation from acceptable behavior, and the need for a very radical examination of your life. A murderer, or a child-abuser would hopefully sooner or later feel that kind of remorse.

Inappropriate guilt hangs on forever, paralyzing you with "if-only's" and "what-if's." A friend told me, "I have a round-trip ticket on the guilt train. Anytime it rolls through the station, I climb aboard!" Another friend quipped, "I never get off—station or not!"

Where Do We Get on the Guilt Train?

Children are keenly attuned to the emotional vibrations of their parents and other adults. Children are exquisitely sensitive barometers of family feelings. From birth to the age of six or seven, children are not merely sensitive but also very self-centered. At that age they are incapable of understanding outside causes; thus, whenever something happens in the home, in their minds, they caused it. When my oldest son was five years old he said to me, "Mommy, please don't cry! When you cry, I feel like I've killed someone."

I knew how my son felt because as a little girl, I wore French braids and every morning, as my mother did my hair, she sighed repeatedly. Times were tough—my father was

125

away at war, money was tight, my mother had to work, and I was left in the care of an unloving grandmother. To my little heart and mind, each of those sighs and the feelings behind them meant that I was a burden: *I* was making my mother unhappy. A generation later my son felt the tears I was shedding over his dad and my divorce were *his* fault.

Through much of my adult life, it upset me terribly whenever anyone sighed. I immediately felt guilty and experienced a tremendous urge to make them feel better, or to run away. Telling myself how silly that was brought no relief until I realized that the roots of my underlying assumption lay in those early hair-braiding sessions with my mother. As a child, I had lacked the awareness and sophistication to simply ask Mother if it bothered her to braid my hair; I could only take clues and fit them into my child's narrow reality. My underlying assumption became: I'm a burden. I need to make other people happy, because it's my fault if they're not.

How do we get off the guilt train? By reminding ourselves that we aren't responsible for other people's happiness.

It took me a long time to convince my guilt-prone inner child that she really didn't need to punish herself with inappropriate guilt feelings. With gentle, patient, persistent reminders, she came around to believing me. Now, she can relax and let others carry their own responsibilities. Every time something happens that would have made me feel guilty in the past, and I don't, I feel exhilarated and free.

Talking to others about our feelings is very helpful in resolving guilt. It's amazing how quickly guilt can melt away when we receive loving feedback from other people who, because they're less involved, can be more objective about what's happening to us.

The last time I saw the friend who'd said she had a round-trip ticket on the guilt train, she told me she no longer felt guilty. I was intrigued and sent her a card with a picture of a bewildered little figure carrying a suitcase. It said: "I'm going on a guilt trip. Would you mind dropping by to feed my paranoia?" Her response was: "I don't mind feeding your paranoia anytime—since I stopped feeding (or feeding on) my own guilt, I have more time for such good deeds." She had made a conscious decision to stop feeling guilty, and she succeeded. So can you.

Anger and Resentment

Scratch a woman and you find a rage.
-Virginia Woolf

Another pile of dirt that gets swept under our emotional carpet consists of anger and resentment. Anger is, for women, the ultimate taboo. We were taught not to be angry, and if we were, to definitely not express it. We learned to mask our anger, to express it in covert ways, or to dutifully hold it in until all hell breaks loose.

Stress research has established that suppressed or inappropriately expressed anger comes out in many forms, including withdrawal, ulcerated colons, migraines, child abuse, depression, and suicide.

Patricia Sun, a teacher of spirituality and conscious living, says, "Anger is our intuitive, right brain telling us, 'Whoops, something's not right here!'" Anger is a warning device. To resolve it wisely, first pay attention to it. You don't have to do all the things your emotionally charged feelings suggest to you: I'm going to hit him with a baseball bat! And of course you shouldn't hurt anyone; but anger, if not allowed to fester and grow out of proportion, is healthy, like a smoke alarm that can prevent all sorts of damage.

We ignore our anger primarily because we don't want to rock the boat. Of course, there are usually more specific reasons: we've been punished for being angry; we've been rejected for not acting nice; and so on. When our conditioning prevails, anger smolders into resentment. Resentment becomes an out-of-control, irrational force, which casts blame on others.

Rebecca was married to the same man for fifty years. She was angry many times but only rarely expressed her feelings. When she and her husband established their patterns of married behavior, assertiveness wasn't popular. Whenever she tried to express her anger, her husband reacted with one short verbal blast and then withdrew into icy silence that lasted for days or even weeks.

Rebecca was no dummy. She learned not to say what she was feeling. But her unexpressed anger turned into smoldering resentment, which during her fifty years of marriage expressed itself as accidents, ulcers, loss of interest in sex, and finally fatal cancer. Rebecca died blaming her husband for ruining her life through his uncaring attitude.

Because of the general advances in awareness initiated by the women's movement, we're more cognizant now that it's okay to be angry, and that it's natural to express our anger. We have a right to be angry; but with that right comes a responsibility to express our anger constructively. If you express your anger in nonconstructive ways, you set yourself up to feel guilty, thus creating more debris instead of removing some. In this case, *constructive* means "not destructive."

Not expressing your anger is unhealthy. Some of us are better than others at keeping the lid on, but sooner or later we blow it. I like the image of a pressure cooker: the pressure builds up and the food inside gets cooked quickly, but if you don't remember to open the little valve on top so the steam can escape in a controlled manner—stand back, 'cause there's going to be dinner all over the ceiling!

Once you've allowed pressure to build up to the point where it can only blow, you can't express yourself constructively. So, once again, the trick is to become *aware* of your anger and resentment. There it is, whether you want it or not, and it's trying to tell you something. *Acknowledge* your feelings to someone who can help you sort through them. It doesn't have to be the person with whom you're upset, in fact, sometimes that's exactly the wrong person to talk to because, in the heat of the moment, you may say something that will cause lasting damage—or the person you're talking to may be the kind who can't listen. Now *accept* that you have a right to your anger and know that it's there to guide you. If you express your anger constructively, you won't need to experience resentment or guilt.

Anger can become a valuable tool when you learn to express it well. Step back from the feelings a bit and ask yourself what you want to accomplish with your anger. Do you want to reconnect with a person? Right a wrong? Understand a situation better? Be understood? Free yourself from a harmful relationship?

It's never helpful to hurt or abuse a person physically or emotionally under the influence of anger (or at any other time). But there are constructive ways to release pent-up anger. When you're steaming, it's a good idea to release the unmanageable excess anger before you confront the person you're angry with. No one reacts receptively to a full-face blast from the dragon's fiery jaws. An angry frontal attack puts even the most invulnerable person on the defensive.

I like to beat beds with a tennis racket—especially the bed of the person I'm angry with (when they're not in it, of course! and preferably not even home). I know women who go out driving on the freeway and scream or who throw eggs at trees. These methods may sound a little weird, but they work! (And are lots of fun for those of us who've spent a lifetime trying to be nice girls.) Anger creates steam, and it's only constructive to release it one manageable piece at a time so

129

that nobody gets scalded.

Carol releases her anger in a way that helps her local charities. She goes to a thrift store, buys a bunch of old china, goes to the dump and throws plates, cups, and saucers as far and as hard as she can. The dump is a great place for her crockery-smashing sessions, because she doesn't feel guilty about making a mess and she doesn't have to clean up afterward. Her teenage daughter likes to go with her. Carol has been able to give herself and her daughter permission to have anger toward her ex-husband, who deserted them, and to express that anger constructively. She and her daughter usually end up laughing together—a wonderfully healing conclusion.

It isn't appropriate to voice your feelings to the people concerned if you think that: you'll come away the loser; you won't be heard; you'll damage a relationship beyond repair; or, you'll jeopardize your job. In such cases, it's wiser to choose not to talk to the person.

Years ago, when I was going through my divorce and my whole life was up for review, I went through a period of feeling intense anger toward my parents. Fortunately, I chose not to share my feelings with them but rather to release those feelings in other ways, like poison-pen letters that were *never* sent, and with other people. Why was that fortunate? Because as I became clear about the source of my anger, I found it didn't have as much to do with my parents as I'd thought. Sure, I'd had my share of hurts in childhood—we all have. If I had blasted my parents with the full force of my anger, I might have fractured our relationship irreparably. They didn't deserve to be made the targets for all the rage and frustration I was feeling over my divorce and the events that had led up to it. However, I did choose understanding friends with whom to share my rage.

If suppressed, repressed, or destructively expressed, anger, like a gun turned against the holder, can cripple us. If

130

used constructively, it can be very empowering. Outrage only harms us when it becomes *in*rage.

Unresolved Grief

Grief is a process. If it is allowed, healing will take place naturally.
     -Hospice of the Foothills

No matter how rich our life or how bright our future, we all experience grief. To live is to change and be vulnerable to loss. Loss brings grief. Unresolved grief takes so much strength to suppress that we have little energy left over for other things—like becoming ourselves and freeing ourselves from emotional dependence. Adopting new patterns of behavior and attitudes happens best when we are not burdened with the debris of unresolved grief. Carrying old grief keeps us in a *re*action rut rather than an action mode.

Since none of us escapes grief, it is important we learn healthy ways to grieve. Natural grieving is allowing ourselves to experience our feelings and move through them at the time of loss. This process is cleansing and leads to full recovery and, often, an enhancement of spirituality and compassion is our reward.

Unresolved grief is created when we don't allow ourselves to work through feelings as they arise. Often we totally deny we even have painful feelings. So we shelve them. But they don't simply evaporate; they gnaw at our energy, prey on our emotions, and generally debilitate us.

Grief comes in many forms. Grief over death and loss is just one. Another is grief over the things we feel we should have done or shouldn't have done. When we fight with a friend or mate, we grieve. When too many bills pile up and money is tight, we grieve. Allowing ourselves to get so busy

131

we can't enjoy life is a pervasive grief for those of us who need to "do it all." Anything unfinished and left to fester becomes emotional debris, the litter of unresolved grief.

Many of us allow emotional debris to collect in our hearts, minds, and souls. Soon the mounds of debris that we've swept under our emotional carpets become too big to ignore. They keep us from walking around freely in our own inner homes and separate us from those we care about. Those mounds soon erode our freedom to make conscious choices about who we are and how we want to be in the world.

In order to heal and become our authentic selves we must recognize and unravel the pain of grief. When the pain of grief winds itself around your heart, don't try to "pull yourself up by you bootstraps" and tough it out. You will only accumulate debris by refusing to face your pain honestly and courageously.

Talk. Share your pain. Cry over it. Read about loss and grieving, join a group, and be especially careful of your body, which is weaker and more vulnerable when you are grieving. Pace yourself to recovery; don't try to do business as usual. Realize, while you are healing from a loss, that you've been hit by an emotional truck or, if it's a small loss, by a VW Bug. You may need to grieve for five minutes, five weeks, or in diminishing intensity, for five years. But time is a healer and, though it may hardly seem possible while you grieve, if you allow yourself to move through grief, you *will* heal.

Isolation

As I begin to understand each of my clients more deeply, I hear a silent plea echoing behind their spoken words of pain: see me, hear me, hold me. All of us need the close contact and validation of our fellow humans. We are social beings, and when we don't experience such contact, we feel isolated and unfulfilled.

As a therapist, I see the ravages of isolation daily. People who've been unable to share their concerns with understanding friends or families feel a chronic isolation that gathers like huge piles of unresolved emotional debris, and turns eventually into life-threatening despair.

A certain amount of solitude is essential. Isolation is something completely different. We need to feel we are a part of the groups with which we live and work, to feel attached to, and to identify with them—not in a dependent relationship but in a grounded, mutually helpful way. Churches, families, schools, self-help groups, and friends all help us overcome feelings of isolation.

Many of us began to feel isolated early in life; when our parents misunderstood, criticized, teased, or judged us, we began to fear sharing ourselves with others. The world felt unsafe. If our parents didn't see, hear, or hold us, or if they loved us only when we were doing things right, we began to feel that even if it were safe to share our real feelings, we weren't worthy to do so. We became adults who didn't want to burden others with our troubles, or air our dirty laundry in public. But we pay dearly for our silence. Isolation is a form of emotional suicide.

People in the bereavement groups I lead are astounded by how much better they feel once they share their pain with others and learn that they are not alone or unique in their reactions. Their isolation is broken, connections form, and healing begins.

Frequently in our isolation we feel unaccepted and unacceptable. We think we're different, the only ones who feel a certain way. Everyone else looks squared-away and happy; we're the weird ones. We develop a socially suitable facade behind which we hide our true feelings. We become social chameleons, changing to suit different situations and people. To some extent, all of us do this because we all feel frightened to reveal how vulnerable we are in certain situations.

Dr. Pauline Rose Clance, in her book, *The Imposter Phenomenon: Overcoming the Fear that Haunts Your Success*, shows that none of us have a flawless self-concept. She writes: "I constantly see men and women (especially women) who have every right to be on top of the world, but instead they're miserable because in their eyes they never measure up. They feel fraudulent."

No matter how successful we are, or how loved, many of us hear a whispering, convincing voice inside that reminds us of our faults and failings. The way to transform that inner saboteur is to learn to love and accept ourselves *as we are*. We need to come to an understanding of the part of us that is judgmental and tries so terribly hard to be perfectionistic. Madame Marie Curie said, "Nothing in life is to be feared. It is only to be understood." In our confusion, we fear that our faults and weaknesses are unforgivable, so we isolate ourselves behind a mask and never move beyond it into the freedom of understanding. No wonder we have difficulty being ourselves!

Breaking out of isolation takes courage. If your isolation is a long-standing habit, give yourself time to go forward slowly and safely.

Victoria, a victim of violent sexual child abuse, protected herself and others from her terrifying secret for many years. Even now, she only feels safe talking about her traumatic experiences only if her legs are drawn up tightly under her chin. Her physical withdrawal reflects her emotional withdrawal. If she gives herself that safety now, a day will come when she'll feel comfortable talking in a more relaxed position.

If we aren't gentle and kind to ourselves as we risk change, we merely reinforce the conviction that the world isn't a safe place and, therefore, we'd better not take the gamble of being our authentic selves.

Explore the reasons why you isolate yourself. What are you protecting? What do you fear? Find people with whom you can take off your mask—people who're willing to see, hear, and hold you. By all means, avoid throwing your (emotional) pearls before swine. Swine are people who say things like, "You shouldn't feel that way" or, "That's stupid—why don't you just ____?" Swine make you wish you'd kept your mouth shut. Be discerning about those with whom you take off your protective mask. You very much need—and deserve—empathetic, kind understanding.

Remind yourself that you carry around an inner child who feels that being isolated is the only safe way to live. Why is she frightened? Can she count on you to protect her? Be a loving parent to your inner child.

Moving beyond inner isolation also helps us give up being a Designated Doormat and Responsibility Sponge for everyone.

Become loving and honest with yourself, too. None of us is perfect! We all have our share of inner squiggly worms (and some boa constrictors). The more we can honestly and gently be vulnerable with others, the more we can free ourselves from our fears and foibles. The freer we are from fear the less emotionally dependent we become.

Writing the first edition of this book was risky and scary for me. For months I wouldn't let anybody read it. When I mailed the first chapters to my business manager, my stomach felt as if it had been shoved in the mailbox too. But it has turned out to be a healing outlet for fears and limitations that I've experienced for years.

Do yourself a transformative favor: find a creative outlet for your pain. One of the best ways to sweep away old fear-debris and break isolation is to reach out in honesty, love, and service to someone else—not because we "should" or as a bitter sacrifice, but as an invitation to a loving bond and a mutual boost to ourselves and the other person.

Part Three

Healing: Owning Your Own Excellence

CHAPTER 10

Beyond Fear: Transforming The Dragons

Our strength is often composed of the weaknesses we're damned if we're going to show.

-Mignon McLaughlin

Now that we have explored many of the ways in which and reasons why we women get trapped in emotional dependence, let's look at how we can move beyond fear and limiting patterns of behavior by transforming our inner dragons and owning our own excellence. As we become able to honor ourselves and our process, we move ever closer to healthy independence.

How do parents encourage the infant who's just learning to walk? They hold her hand, provide a safe environment, and congratulate each new success.

Similarly, in moving beyond fear, realize that you must go forward at a beginner's pace. Take baby steps. Be proud of each faltering toddle, each newly taken footstep. Become a kind and encouraging parent to yourself. Gently congratulate yourself on your successes, and comfort yourself after your failures.

Self-hate never does any good. How often have you said to yourself, I just hate my fear of rejection, or, I just hate myself when I overeat. Did hating yourself ever decrease your fear of rejection (or your waistline) by a single millimeter? Take a second now to go back and read those two self-hating statements. Notice where the power lies: I just hate my fear of rejection translates to: I am afraid of rejection—I affirm it, and hate it.

Self-hate drives its object even deeper into our consciousness. Why not try a little experiment: the next time you're tempted to feel self-hate, whether it's for pigging out before bedtime or letting someone dominate you, try the Love and Acceptance Cure. Who, exactly, is expecting you to hate yourself for what happened? No one! Talk to yourself in a spirit of love and acceptance. Be on your own side. Sure, you could have done better, but what you need right now is a good friend—yourself—to laugh gently and encourage you.

Talk to yourself. It's by no means crazy—we do it all the time anyway. But talk nicely! Would your pets cringe and whimper if you talked to them in the way you've been talking to yourself? Create an internal atmosphere of love and acceptance so you'll have the courage to become aware of your fears and feelings.

An interesting study, written about several years ago in *Psychology Today,* reported that several sports psychologists had compared world-class athletes with athletes who were never quite able to fulfill their potential. The difference, they discovered, was that the world-class athletes were able to forgive their mistakes immediately and carry on, while second-class athletes browbeat themselves whenever they made a mistake. This research underscores the idea that the ability to forgive ourselves is rewarded with success, while feeling guilty and beating up on ourselves is penalized with failure.

Negativity never heals negativity. As a wise person once said, "You can't get rid of the darkness by beating at it with a stick. You must turn on the light."

Steps Toward Transformation

Become *aware* of the dragons and fears inside you. If you

understand your feelings and allow them to just be there without judging them, they'll move on, heal, and become transmuted. If you fearfully resist them, labeling them bad/ wrong/ugly, they'll stick to your mind and grow. *Acknowledge* your feelings. You don't need to act on them; just see them. Invite your dragons into the light—take a dragon to lunch. Then, *accept* them. Feelings aren't right or wrong; they just *are*. A gentle climate of love and acceptance fosters healing and growth.

Change is action; old habits are reactions. To change and transform we must consciously choose new actions. All the buried patterns we've talked about so far are ingrained, passive, fixed, change-resisting reactions to people and circumstances. The only way to be free of them is to create fresh, new actions to replace them. We need to *act* rather than *react*. As we learn to break out of the cycle of reaction we become better able to be who we really are.

As I have been discussing throughout the book, the steps outlined above are the basic tools of change. Now let me share with you a somewhat wider perspective on self-change.

Understand, Pause, Choose

Step 1: Awareness, Acknowledgment, and Acceptance
Bring into the open old patterns, reactions, or fears.

Step 2: Pause
Before you act, step back, take time out—a breather—to gain perspective. You can't see much with your nose pressed right up against what you're looking at. Examine your feelings; then compare your options: remember how you have reacted in the past. Is it appropriate now or would you rather choose other deliberate, creative, healing actions?

Step 3: Choose

This step is crucial! By pausing, you've taken yourself off automatic pilot so you are free to decide on a new course of action. How would you like to act? If the old reaction isn't working, choose to act in a different way. You don't have to continue old patterns. You are now in the driver's seat.

If you take a single word out of this book and make it your own on a day-to-day basis, I hope it's *choose*. If you can *choose* to act in a different way, even while feeling the old way, you'll find it tremendously liberating!

Once, when my husband and I were having a confrontation in which I felt judged and rejected, I recognized an old reaction pattern, a three-phase dance I used to go into whenever I felt threatened: First, I'd feel guilty and wrong for "making" him unhappy, so I'd become jovial and conciliatory in order to jolly him out of his mood. When that didn't work, I became the counselor-in-residence and (oh, so calmly) pointed out the error of his ways, reasonably citing the various psychological bases of the misunderstanding. That *never* worked. No one, especially our mate, is ever very receptive to being "enlightened" concerning the reasons for his or her irrational behavior while they're in the midst of feeling hurt, angry, or frustrated.

When neither of those tactics worked, I became frustrated, lonely, and discouraged. I would withdraw into righteous anger and slog around in a cloud of resentment and disappointment. Obviously, my mood was his fault. Why couldn't he be different? I had fallen into my victim role.

During this particular episode, before the familiar pattern got into full swing, I *paused* and asked myself some very important questions:

1. *Have these reactions worked in the past?*
2. *Do I feel better when I react in these ways?*

3. Is our relationship better after I've gone through the old, familiar reactions?

In each case, the answer was a resounding "No!" So the next question was obvious:

4. Do I still want to react this way?

Now, having paused and stepped back from my feelings, I could *choose* how I would act.

I decided to detach myself—to withdraw from the events that were taking place—not in anger, resentment, or with a feeling of rejection, but in order to let him take responsibility for his own feelings.

I shut myself up with my tape recorder and made some notes for this book and another one. Instead of trying to convince my husband to change, I changed. I stepped out of the victim role, the overly responsible role, and the I-must-be-wrong emotionally dependent role, and took care of myself.

From the neck up, I was exhilarated by the change in my behavior, but my body continued to behave in the old way. My stomach churned and a giant talon seized my throat. My body felt guilty, rejected, scared, and lonely all at the same time.

I talked to my body and to my scared inner child, telling them that I would take care of them. I encouraged myself to relax and kept assuring myself that I was safe and that I no longer needed the old feelings to protect me. Very slowly, my body began to get the message. After a few hours, the exhilaration in my head percolated through my entire body and I felt great!

I had been true to myself, taken charge of my reactions, and turned an old dragon into a new and better way of relating to my husband. A very freeing experience! It was healing for him also since the old pattern had always created resentment and hostility toward him. My new pattern of action freed us both from having to deal with that.

We need to entice our personal fear dragons out of their dark caves. When we can work up the courage to do that, we'll begin moving toward greater and greater emotional freedom. As our dragons come into the light of awareness and as our willingness and ability to face and heal inner fears increases, we'll be able to replace old dragons with new patterns and as a result have wonderful experiences of fresh inner freedom.

CHAPTER 11

The Power Of Thought

As a matter of fact, we are always affirming something, be it for good or ill. We are always either saying, I can" or "I cannot." What we need to do is to eliminate the negative and accentuate the positive. In doing this we shall gradually acquire the habit of affirmative thinking.

-Ernest Holmes

Wise people throughout the ages have spoken of the tremendous power of human thought:

Marcus Aurelius:
Our life is what our thoughts make it."

Solomon:
"As a man thinketh, so is he."

Buddha:
"All that we are is the result of what we have thought."

William James:
"Belief creates the actual fact."

Ralph Waldo Emerson:
"What a man thinks of himself, that is which determines, or rather indicates, his fate."

Henry Ford:
"Whether you think you can or think you can't, you're right."

Thinking Is The Birth Of Feeling

The last of the human freedoms is to choose one's attitude in any given set of circumstances.
-Victor Frankl

We generally keep more than one thought track going at the same time in our minds. Some are closer to the surface of consciousness than others. But we are constantly talking to ourselves. This is called "self-talk."

Listen to what you're saying to yourself in the privacy of your own mind. If what you habitually tell yourself is optimistic, uplifting, and loving, you're certain to be a person who feels happy and energized. If the tone of your thoughts is self-recriminating, resistant, or negative, you'll inevitably feel down and depressed. Thinking is the birth of feeling.

Negative, fearful self-talk undermines your self-esteem, creates painful feelings, and renders emotional independence almost unattainable. One of the quickest ways to become anxious is to let yourself worry about the future. I call this falling in the future hole. Future Hole self-talk statements often start out, "What if . . . "; "I couldn't handle . . . "; "I'm afraid that . . . ".

Our minds, if undisciplined, wander off easily from the here and now into projections of the future. We need to plan for the future, but not worry. Planning creates security; worry creates pain. Planning is empowering; worrying accentuates helplessness.

Check your self-talk: How do you speak to yourself? Are you kind and encouraging? Would you talk similarly to a close friend? How are your thoughts contributing to your feelings? In positive ways or negative ways? It isn't circumstance that creates our feelings; it's our *thoughts* about circumstances that give birth to our feelings.

Carrie had been unhappy in her marriage for a long time. She often said, "I wish Bill would just leave!" Finally, Bill left, and Carrie fell apart. In her fear and grief about being alone, she forgot how unhappy they had been together and only concentrated on how awful she felt that he was gone. She couldn't handle being abandoned, and she blamed herself totally. Her pain, which was natural, was increased by her self-talk. The circumstance Carrie had in fact desired was now made unbearable by what she was telling herself about it. Her resistance so magnified her pain that she began to drink heavily to escape her feelings.

Carrie could have healed more quickly by becoming aware of her victimizing self-talk and choosing to replace it with supportive positive affirmations. For example, every time she found herself repeating the old, painful litany, she could have said, "I am strong and able to handle all circumstances that come my way!"

Your feelings, and the thoughts that created them, are your own responsibility, nobody else's. Take responsibility (not blame!) for changing your *thoughts*, if you want to change your feelings. When you choose to change your thoughts, you cease to be a victim. As your thoughts and feelings become more positive, supportive, and life-affirming, your experience of life will be freer. You'll be encouraged to be yourself.

What You Think You Are, You Will Become

The unleased power of the atom has changed everything except our modes of thinking, and we thus drift toward unparalleled catastrophes.
-Albert Einstein

Imagine your mind as a garden. Which thoughts will you plant in it? Negative, unhealthy, self-critical thoughts are like weeds. When you plant positive, healthy, constructive thoughts, you can expect a crop of beautiful flowers. Thus you alone determine whether your life looks like an overgrown weed patch or a well-tended, lushly beautiful flower garden.

If you've allowed your mind to drift along as it pleases for a long time (and most of us have), you'll need to train yourself gradually to become a healthy thinker. It helps to think of negative thoughts as unsettling music playing on the radio; you have the power to turn the dial to music you find enjoyable and soothing. You are just as able to change the dial on your negative self-talk! Tune in without judgment to what you are thinking. If your thinking isn't leading your life toward healthy attitudes and positive feelings, change the station.

Changing our thoughts is simple, which is not to say it's easy. No habit is easy to break, and unhealthy thinking is one of the most stubborn habits of all, one we may have built up over a lifetime. We need to have faith, though: what we've done, we can patiently undo. It will take practice and perseverance, but believe me, it is worth the challenge! Very simply, we choose to change our thinking, and then we formulate a plan of action. Here's an example from my life:

When I started to write this book, it became very clear to me that I was running full speed into my fears of failure. In school I had always dreaded writing themes and essays, and the thought of writing a *book* terrified me. On the day I was to meet the literary agent for the first time, I used hair spray instead of deodorant and lost my car in the parking lot where I'd parked for two years. I was completely spaced out, and no wonder. At the time, my dominant self-talk was: What in the world do you think you're doing! You can't write! You got C's in English (I hadn't, but I felt as if I had). You must be crazy! *You* don't have anything to say.

My mind was full of extremely unhealthy self-talk—in fact, my mind had become my enemy. I felt anxious and disoriented. I decided to change my thoughts. I tentatively assured myself that I did have something to say. After all, I had spent years as a working therapist and had achieved a great deal using the ideas I proposed to write about. I began to feel less anxious . . . or so I thought.

I arrived at my office for my first scheduled writing marathon without my research files, notes, tape recorder, and very important tapes. All of this stuff—my book!—was scattered all over the road, since I had left it on top of the car when I drove off.

Why was I sabotaging myself? I realized I was afraid that if I failed, I'd look stupid and I'd have wasted a lot of time. If I succeeded, people might be jealous, and I still had a lot of memories about high school and family issues concerning jealousy. Could an "ordinary" girl like me do something "exceptional" like be an author?

> *I never realized until lately that women were supposed to be the inferior sex.*
> -Katherine Hepburn

Unlike Miss Hepburn, I had realized we were supposed to be inferior! The book was pushing me out of my comfort zone, across limits beyond which I couldn't very well continue to function if I felt inferior. I was going to have to risk.

I began to take the project more lightly. Someone once said, "Angels fly because they take themselves lightly." I had been taking writing so seriously I could hardly walk, let alone fly. I decided to **SOAR: Stretch Out And Risk**. I decided I would enjoy the writing while I did it and have fun being an author. Having chosen to think differently, I began to put into effect some well-chosen positive affirmations.

Develop into a Healthy Thinker

The select few who've mastered the art of meditation can empty their minds; the rest of us can't stop thinking, and much of what we think isn't at all conducive to happiness. Therefore, when we catch ourselves thinking negatively, we need to plan a script of thoughts to replace our unhealthy self-talk.

Avoid the error of chastising yourself for negative thinking. If you catch yourself in the middle of some particularly negative self-talk and berate yourself: There I go again! How terrible! No wonder I feel as I do! Why can't I stop this?, you'll only start a new line of negative, self-critical thoughts. Instead, give yourself a gold star for a good job of vigilant thought monitoring.

I watch my self-talk carefully. I was recently working with a client who's suicidal. After the session I noticed I was feeling depressed and on the verge of tears. I tuned in to my self-talk. I'd been saying, I should be able to save her! If she dies, I'll be responsible. I can't stand it if she doesn't get well! No wonder I felt lousy.

I checked the reality of those debilitating thoughts and began to replace them with: She is a child of God, safe in the universe; I am a good therapist; I love myself and her. I pictured her well and happy. I began to feel better. Sad, still, but then it was a sad situation. But I changed the statements that were giving me pain and began to release my feelings of failure and fear, which would have become obstacles to my helping her.

Affirmations are flower seeds that we plant in our subconscious. They have a powerful effect in helping us build a life that is happy, authentic, and free from fear. Conscious affirmations are an effective means of reprogramming negative self-talk, underlying assumptions, and hidden attitudes.

Probably the most important affirmation you can have is: I love myself. If you simply can't say that, try: I am willing to love myself, or, I am willing to be willing to love myself. Whenever you become aware of unhealthy self-talk, replace it with one of the following affirmations, or create your own affirmations to meet your particular needs:

Positive Self-Talk Affirmations

1. *I love myself.*
2. *I am a good friend to myself and others.*
3. *I am a creative and worthwhile person even though I make mistakes.*
4. *I know my limits and boundaries and stand up for them in a firm and loving manner.*
5. *I now have time, energy, wisdom, and money to accomplish all that I desire.*
6. *I am powerful in my life.*
7. *I am now willing to be my ideal weight and have my ideal appearance.*
8. *I am a valuable and important person, and I am worthy of the love and respect of others.*
9. *I have satisfying and supportive relationships.*
10. *I feel creative and valued in my work.*

Your Own Affirmations: Flower Seed Sentences

To be effective, affirmations need to be in the present tense. Write your affirmations as if they were true *now*:
1.
2.
3.
4.
5.

We not only become what we think; we become what we picture and feel. While repeating your affirmations, picture the realities behind them as clearly and in as much detail as possible. If you're affirming that you're a worthwhile person, close your eyes and see or sense a picture of yourself being appreciated by others; or look in the mirror and tell yourself eye to eye how valuable and worthwhile you are. If you receive a note or card of appreciation, carry it with you and look at it often.

Don't expect quick results. You are re-programming your subconscious mind—the most complex computer on earth. It will take time for your feelings to catch up with your new thoughts. But even if you don't feel the truth of the affirmation now, know that real work is being done on a subconscious level. This has been proven true over and over again by people who faithfully, persistently practice affirmations. These include world-class athletes and successful business people.

Think of the process of reprogramming your self-talk as being similar to training a puppy to the leash. At first, the puppy digs in its paws, puts its head down, and refuses to budge. Once it gets used to the idea, it runs ahead eagerly, enjoying the experience. Our feelings are comparable: once our self-talk becomes self-loving and healthy, our feelings will surge ahead, freer and happier.

You may hear an insidious internal voice, sneering at your efforts and discounting any possibility of this dumb exercise working. It'll tell you you're bound to fail. It'll try to make you feel hopeless and helpless. It'll negate your right to be happy. It'll tell you that affirmations are too simple to be effective.

The following exercise is a good one for exorcising the internal Discounter who stands over our shoulder and says, "Oh yeah!? Wanna bet!? Not on your life!"

Take a blank sheet of paper and *print* carefully in the left column your affirmation; then in the right column quickly *write* any negative response from the Discounter. Continue carefully printing the same affirmation in the left column and quickly dashing off all negative comments in the right column until you've exhausted the Discounter. Now you are ready to use your affirmation unhindered by your own inner saboteur.

Self-Talk Discounter Exorcism

Affirmation (print carefully)	Negative Responses (write quickly)
1. I love myself.	You've got to be kidding.
2. I love myself.	Why? No one else does!
3. I love myself.	You don't deserve love!
4. I love myself.	You've done a lot of awful things.
5. I love myself.	You aren't spiritual enough.
6. I love myself.	Maybe a little, sometimes.
7. I love myself.	But you're 20 pounds overweight! You'll be lovable when you lose them.
8. I love myself.	You make so many mistakes . . . but you try hard.
9. I love myself.	I'm tired of writing this . . .
10. I love myself.	Okay, okay . . . .
11. I love myself.	I do love myself . . . yes, I deserve love.

Use your affirmations faithfully. Choose how you will think. Picture yourself already experiencing the circumstances or attitudes you're affirming. You'll begin to experience the freedom of being yourself.

The Power Of Thought

Your mind is a sacred enclosure into which nothing harmful can enter except by your permission.
-Arnold Bennett

You are in charge of what enters your mind. When worries plague you, put them on what my dad calls his "2:00 a.m. Worrying List." Being a very sound sleeper, he rarely gets to that list.

Read only materials that feed your soul and uplift your thoughts. Be with people who are positive, optimistic, and happy. Find ways to protect yourself from absorbing negative "vibes." Don't subject yourself to negative TV and movie fare. You may feel unaffected, but your subconscious will carry the ideas (and fears) around for days, perhaps even years. It is junk food for the mind.

You can plant thought-seeds of lack, in which case you'll end up believing in and experiencing lack; or you can plant thought-seeds of plenty. It's up to you: you can believe in your limitations, or you can believe that you can soar.

My son is a good example of the power of belief. His lifelong ambition was to be a professional athlete. During his senior year in high school, his right knee was severely injured and he was told by an orthopedic surgeon that he'd never play sports again, and that there was a good chance he'd walk with a limp for the rest of his life. My son and I refused to believe in that limitation and we searched until we found a knee specialist who gave us hope. Two years and three surgeries later, he completed his first triathlon race: a one-and-a-half-mile swim, a fifty-mile bike ride, and a thirteen and a-half-mile marathon run. He chose to believe he could, and he did! You can too!

CHAPTER 12

Yes,
We Do Have Rights

*Helmer: Remember—before all else you
are a wife and mother.
Nora: I don't believe that anymore. I
believe that before all else I am a
human being, just as you are.*

-Henrik Ibsen

A Bill of Rights for Women

1. I have the right to be treated with respect.
2. I have the right to have and express my feelings and opinions.
3. I have the right to be listened to and taken seriously.
4. I have the right to set my own priorities.
5. I have the right to say No without feeling guilty.
6. I have the right to ask for the things I want and need.
7. I have the right to be different than others expect me to be.
8. I have the right to make my own choices.
9. I have the right to laugh and have fun.
10. I have the right to love and be loved.
11. I have the right to be paid fairly for what I do.
12. I have the right to be happy.

*T*he above list was compiled from many long-forgotten sources; the one source I do remember is my own life. In my journey toward independence, I've struggled with each of these issues.

When you read the list, what's your response? If you can say, "Yes, I believe that—I have those rights in my life now," you have gone beyond dependence and have achieved the courage to be yourself.

But do some of the items make you shake your head and say, "You've got to be kidding! I could never feel that way! Even if I did, my family and friends would never honor it!" If so, read on.

It really is true that we teach people how to treat us. Before we can expect to be treated well, we must believe we deserve good treatment. Before we can have our rights respected, we must believe that we have rights.

To convince yourself that you do have rights, remind yourself constantly of those rights. Post a copy of the above list, or a list of your own making, in a prominent place in your house and workplace, where it'll serve two purposes: it'll remind you what you're working toward, implanting positive ideas in your subconscious mind; and it'll make others aware of what you're striving for.

Kristy worked full-time, yet her husband and two sons expected her to assume full responsibility for the household as well. She went on strike—not just for a day or a week, but for three months. She shopped, cooked, and washed for herself but not for her family. Previously, she'd been feeling victimized by her situation and unable to come up with a good solution; so she became increasingly resentful and angry. When she realized, Yes, I have rights, too! and went on strike, the angry feelings disappeared.

Kristy was willing to risk her family's displeasure. At first, she took a lot of flak. Her husband and sons teased and humored her, thinking she was kidding; by the second week they were furious because they could see how much they'd been demanding, and they knew they were going to have to change. Her strike succeeded; Kristy now has three willing co-workers.

Risk: Taking Responsibility And Making Creative Choices

We are all determined by the fact that we have been born human, and hence by the never-ending task of having to make choices. We must choose the means

together with the aims. We must not rely on anyone's saving us, but be very aware of the fact that wrong choices make us incapable of saving ourselves.
-Erich Fromm

Growth requires the ability and willingness to risk, of courting the unexpected. Risking is scary, but without risk we will be unable to throw off the chains of emotional dependence.

Each risk we take, each pain we heal, each inner dragon we tame widens the path to freedom for others to follow. I like to think of those women who were brave enough to demand the vote and the right to keep property when they married. They forged a trail in consciousness for the rest of us, just as surely as the pioneers broke trails to the West.

Our new path of consciousness has a few visible, historic landmarks, but for the most part it is an invisible trail, felt more than seen. It has been built and paved by the courage, hopes, and tears and fears of the women who've gone before us. Every risk we take makes it easier for others to summon the courage to risk being themselves. By creating new patterns for our own actions, we create patterns for loving respect of the rights of all, both women and men.

It is not easy to find happiness in ourselves, and it is impossible to find it elsewhere.
-Agnes Repplier

Your life is no one's responsibility but your own. There are many things in your life over which you have no control and for which you aren't responsible; but you are responsible for how you respond to any circumstance. And your response alone determines whether circumstance becomes resolved positively.

When we become response-able—that is, when we learn to choose our responses freely and consciously—we are free to build a life of continued growth and increasing happiness.

For those circumstances in life over which we have no control, such as emotional hurts received in early childhood, we can learn to take responsibility for our need to grieve, and make creative choices regarding how we will do so.

Victoria, about whom I spoke earlier, was the victim of violent sexual abuse from infancy until eighteen years of age. She was not responsible for that early pain, but she *is* responsible for her response and rehabilitation. Victoria *must* grieve; at this point her pain is so great that she simply has no choice. But she is free to choose how she will grieve. Although her struggle is a mighty one, she is risking by experiencing her pain, taking responsibility for her healing, and making creative choices. She is also reaching out to others with similar pain . . . a sure sign of loving healing.

Even if we have not endured trauma as atrocious as Victoria has, all of us bear scars that affect how we lead our lives. We need to take responsibility for treating those old wounds and choosing how we will work to heal them, so that we can move on to better things. Ask yourself: If I took responsibility for this situation in my life and my response to it, how could I alter, heal, avoid, solve, stop, work with, or change it? If you started counting on yourself for solutions, where would you start?

What's the first, tiny baby step that you'll take? Don't worry about the overall dimensions of the process; just take that one small step. If you need moral support, talk with a friend or professional counselor. But do it!

If we persist in thinking that "they" need to change before we can be happy, we'll never get anywhere. Whether "they" are your family, mate, friend, the economy, the weather, a circumstance, or unloving parents, if we rely on them to change our lives for us—good luck! We're stuck! When we realize that we're responsible—not blameworthy, but responsible—for our own lives and happiness, we'll begin building the inner power to change and make creative choices. If, for example, your husband is an alcoholic, you have a choice: either blame the situation and be a victim, or go to Al-Anon or take some other practical step toward healing the situation.

Feeling dull and lifeless? What dragon inside you is keeping your sparkle from shining through to the surface? Choose to take responsibility for healing yourself: risk exploring your life patterns and find out what's going on. Find ways to infuse yourself with enthusiasm. You cannot feel bored, dull, or lifeless, and enthusiastic at the same time.

Every change risks a crisis. As you start changing your responses to circumstances, you'll undoubtedly upset some of the people in your life. People resist change, and they are used to you the way you are. The Chinese character for *crisis* is a combination of the characters for *danger* and *opportunity*. Risking change creates danger to the status quo, but opens up new, freeing opportunities for ourselves, our families, and our friends. Risk may be scary, but it brings tremendous rewards. We need to go for it!

Let's dare to be ourselves, for we do that better than anyone else can.
-Shirley Briggs

It's *your* life; don't waste it. You can chart a path toward a happier life by accepting the fact that you are responsible for changing what needs to be changed, and for choosing a creative course of action that will enhance your life.

Speaking Out Without Blowing Up

I was angry with my friend;
I told my wrath, my wrath did end.
I was angry with my foe;
I told it not, my wrath did grow.
                    -William Blake

Learning to speak up for ourselves is extremely important as we choose risky new actions that may emotionally threaten others. There are two ways to tell our wrath: the constructive and destructive. We've all seen (and probably used) the destructive method, hiding feelings or blowing our tops and spewing out raw emotions in people's faces. The destructive way causes our wrath and the wrath of others to grow, rather than to go.

How can we speak out without blowing up or causing others to blow up?

First, convince yourself that you have the right to speak out. If you need to refresh your memory, refer to the Bill of Rights listed earlier. You may also want to search your consciousness for seed sentences that are preventing others from hearing and respecting your words. One of mine used to be: If you don't have anything nice to say, don't say anything at all. I surrounded myself with friends who'd been trained, as I had, to be afraid of confrontation and honest communication. When I voiced my feelings, and my friends told me that what I had to say wasn't "nice," I believed them. So for years I stuffed my feelings back inside even when I needed to share them, fearing I'd be rejected, labeled a bitch, or rock the boat of my precarious emotional dependence.

Once we believe we have a right to voice our feelings and opinions, we need to learn how to speak out constructively. Speaking out in order to make others see an issue our way, to convince them, or to prove them wrong, is acting destructively. We need to learn to speak out with the goal of *understanding* each other: speaking without blaming, and listening without judging.

Blow Up ... But ...

Blowing up is like taking out the garbage. Our minds create emotional garbage that in turn creates harmful toxins in our bodies; if we don't blow up, and blow off those toxins, chances are we'll "blow in" and create such suppression-related maladies as depression, heart disease, and even cancer. Instead of blowing up, lots of women blow *out*—i.e., get fat. I can always tell when I'm holding something back: I put on weight.

There's an art to blowing up constructively. When our inner dragons have built up a good head of steam, we need to blow it out, so long as we aim it away from people and breakable objects. Little children know innately how to blow up: they fling themselves on the floor and pound and kick. Very rarely do they hurt themselves.

Wise parents and teachers call time outs to allow kids to express themselves. The child can go off by herself and express to her heart's content. Give yourself time out! Take the force of your anger and frustration away from people, and let 'er rip. Only then speak out.

If you really go for it while you blow up, you'll feel tired but cleansed. Robert Frost said, "The best way out is always through." I believe this is true of the emotions.

After taking time out to release excess energy, we can talk and listen constructively with the help of a few simple communication tools.

167

Tools For Constructive Communication

*The best impromptu speeches are those written
well in advance.*
                    -Ruth Gordon

A. Prepare for Communication by:
    1. *Blowing up privately.*
    2. *Clarifying what you're feeling and what you want to
        say:*

        a. Make notes to yourself. A client of mine takes an
        emotional memo to herself, labeled "Memo to Me: I'm
        angry about (____)!" She writes down her feelings and
        puts them in the "IN" basket to be worked out at a more
        convenient time. *Always* come back to those "IN" files,
        if only to see if your feelings are now clear. If you don't
        check back, it's a sign you're wanting to suppress those
        feelings.
        b. Organizing what you want to communicate.
        c. Rehearsing what you intend to say.

Remember, communication isn't guerrilla warfare. The
reason for speaking out is to create love, understanding, and
intimacy.

B. Timing
    I can't stress enough how important timing is to good
communication! It's essential! Many people ruin any chance
for constructive communication by choosing the wrong time
to speak. Those four little words, *we have to talk*, strike terror
in the hearts of people who are afraid of confrontation. If we
add *now!*, we're setting ourselves up to be met defensively.
It's only fair that both parties agree on the time to talk.
    Over the years my husband and I have evolved a system

that works for us. If I want to talk, I tell him I need to talk sometime within the next twenty-four hours. I tell him the subject—in one or two sentences, maximum. Then I let him know just how big a deal it is for me. Since he can choose the time, which needs to be mutually agreeable, he has a sense of being empowered in the process. If I were to jump on him and demand that we talk "right now" he'd feel attacked and defensive. I know, because I've done it—it didn't work!

When he chooses the time, he can gather his thoughts on the subject—he can prepare. Some people find it helps to make regular appointments to discuss anything that has come up, or have a "clear the air" dinner once a week, or perhaps schedule ten or twenty minutes each evening specifically to talk.

C. Communicating

1. *Restate your goal.* Before you start talking, take a few deep breaths, hold hands, and each state your goal for the discussion. What do you hope to gain? Learn? Understand? If you stray from the subject, remind each other.

2. *State how you feel.* As you begin the discussion, what are your fears and physical symptoms? Instead of protecting yourself behind masks of attack, indifference, or bravado, show your vulnerabilities. When I need to talk about something uncomfortable, my body gets very anxious. So I might say, "This is really hard for me. My heart is racing and my stomach is churning. I'm perspiring and my tongue feels as big and dry as a throw rug."

3. *Check your reality.* Sometimes what we perceive from the other person isn't what was intended. Before you react, check out your assumptions: I need a reality check; I feel shut out; are you angry with me? If the answer is yes, you can choose to pursue it now or later. If the answer is no, accept it. If your feeling persists, check it out again.

4. Use "I Messages." These tend to eliminate defensiveness. The formula is: "When you do/say (_____), I feel (_____)." The idea is to express *real feelings*, not judgments or accusations. Use one or two words at most to describe a real feeling. Examples of feelings: hurt, confused, tired, angry, joyful, uncomfortable, abandoned, or excited. Feelings describe what's happening to *you*, rather than a judgment about whatever the other person is doing. Here's an example of a clear "I Message": "When you talk to me in that tone of voice, I feel hurt and angry."

By contrast, "You Messages" point fingers, make judgments, criticize personally, and interpret. The "I Message" above could have been sent as a "You Message": "When you talk to me in that tone of voice, you're doing it just to hurt me!" or, "You make me feel awful. You hurt me!" The silent tag line at the end of a "You Message" is, You bastard, you!

"I Messages" *inform*. "You Messages" *attack*.

Examples:

You Messages	I Messages
You are disgusting and irresponsible when you drink.	When you drink, I feel scared and disgusted.
You are rude and irresponsible not to call when you are going to be late.	I feel like an abandoned kid when you don't call if you are going to be late.
You are an insensitive bully to tease me when you know it hurts me.	When you tease me, I feel helpless and angry.

170

D. NonVerbal Communication

One of my clients was in the hospital after the birth of her son. Her mother-in-law visited her and said, "I saw you had a lot of flowers yesterday, so I brought you something today." She handed her a small, unwrapped cactus still boasting its seventy-nine-cent Safeway price tag. A great nonverbal put-down.

Actions speak louder than words. When our nonverbal messages are out of sync with our words, everyone gets confused. We've all had the experience of being in the presence of someone who was acting so cold that your nose hairs froze, yet when asked what was wrong they said (frostily), "Nothing!" That's a mixed (or double) message.

E. Listening

*It takes two to speak the truth—one to speak,
and another to hear.*
> -Henry David Thoreau

Listening is probably *the* most important part of any communication. Listening leads to understanding and creates a bridge to intimacy. Here's some suggestions to foster good listening.

1. *Allow Pauses.* Before you formulate a response, be sure you've taken time to really hear what your partner has said. Resist the tendency to race ahead of your partner's thoughts, stacking up retort ammunition.

Silent pauses are an essential feature of real communication. If you keep trying to break in while the other person is talking, you are not listening. People can't communicate unless you affirm their worth by allowing them to really be heard. Understanding requires hearing. Relationships thrive on understanding. If you want to have successful relation-ships, listen. Really listen!

2. *Reflect Back*. Restate what you believe your partner has just said. If you've ever played the parlor game of Gossip (also called Telephone), where a message gets passed around a circle by one person whispering it to the next, you know that messages get easily distorted by being mis-heard. Verify that you've heard correctly. Make sure you're both talking about the same issue or feeling. Say something like, "When you said `I guess it would be ok,' for me to go to the movies with Nancy on Friday night, were you asking me not to go?"

Don't assume you know what's meant. You know what they say about *assume:* it makes an "ass" out of "u" and "me."

Reflect. Explore. Make sure you understand. To really listen takes patience and desire. The rewards are well worth it!

Honoring What We Want And Need

Why do women leave home to take their services into the marketplace? Money? For sure. But maybe they felt the need to materialize. You had to have been there to know what it was like to be invisible. To move and not be seen, to talk and not be heard. To have family return to the house every evening and say, "Anyone home?"
    -Erma Bombeck

Have you ever felt invisible? Who alone of all the people you know has the power to make you visible? You! And you'll never be visible unless you honor your wants and needs.

What is it you want and need? Affection? Approval? Love? Hugs? To succeed? To be heard? To have help around the house? Do you ask for help filling those wants and needs, or do you hope people will psychically "know" about them without your asking? That's not fair. Expecting people to read our minds hardly ever gets us what we need.

Simone, a teacher, was going through her second divorce and feeling bereft and worthless. Finally, she worked up the courage to ask for what she needed: lots of hugs and acknowledgment that she was okay, even though twice divorced. She made a badge, which she wore at school. It said: "I need eight hugs a day!" Her willingness to ask for what she wanted sparked a revolution at her school. Soon people were not only hugging her but hugging others as well. A climate of closeness developed among the staff which hadn't existed in the pre-hug days.

Other people can never give us all that we want and need, so we must learn to fill some of our own wants and needs ourselves.

Pat is newly single and needs love and hugs. Her underlying need for affection had its origins in a nonsupportive relationship with her mother, and her separation from her husband only exacerbated her feelings of abandonment. Pat's inner little girl is crying for loving acceptance.

I keep a doll in my office, and when I gave it to Pat to hold, she poured out to it all the love that her inner child craves. I encouraged her to buy herself a doll or teddy bear. Silly as it sounds, it helps. Hugging, holding, talking to an accepting cuddly toy encourages us to develop gentle, healing attitudes toward our inner child. You might try hugging several bears or dolls in the store until you find one that feels just right to you.

Pat's case is a good example of how external objects can help us to explore our inner wants and needs, and to honor them. We have a right to know our needs and fulfill them. We can explore ways to ask for what we need, and learn to fill our own needs ourselves.

Yes, We Do Have Rights

As we gain confidence in our rights and learn to honor our wants and needs, we'll open doors to inner wholeness and health. We'll move beyond dependence and discover the courage to be ourselves. We'll discover and honor our own excellence and encourage others to do the same.

CHAPTER 13

Having
The Courage

*Who knows what women can be when
they are finally free to become
themselves? Who knows what
women's intelligence will contribute
when it can be nourished
without denying love?*

-Betty Friedan

*S*ometimes, all it takes to make great strides toward having the courage to be yourself is giving yourself permission. Too often, we wait around for someone to tell us, "Sure, it's okay for you to be who you really are." But ask yourself: Is there anybody in your life who really has that kind of power over you? No! No one else can give us the go-ahead to change. No one else knows the inner longings, dreams, and fears that struggle within us. Thus, only you can know where and how you should give yourself permission to become authentically yourself.

Growth and personal unfolding begin when we give ourselves permission to *be*. Remember this sentence from the Women's Bill of Rights, "I have the right to be different than others expect me to be." Often there is a period of adjustment after we have made a commitment to be ourselves. It is different for us and for others. They may balk at the new pattern; so might we, actually, but in order to outgrow emotional dependence and be truly ourselves we need to accept the discomfort and stick to our commitment.

These words are written on the tomb of an Anglican bishop who was buried in the crypts of Westminster Abbey in A.D. 1100:

When I was young and free and my imagination had
no limits, I dreamed of changing the world.
As I grew older and wiser, I discovered the world
would not change, so I shortened my sights somewhat
and decided to change only my country.
But it too seemed immovable.
As I grew into my twilight years, in one last
desperate attempt, I settled for changing only my
family, those closest to me, but alas, they would have
none of it.
And now as I lie on my deathbed, I suddenly
realize:
If I had only changed myself first, then by
example I might have changed my family.
From their inspiration and encouragement I would
then have been able to better my country, and who
knows,
I may have even changed the world.

Nobody Said It Would Be Easy

Courage, as this book defines it, is the willingness to act even when frightened. If we've been emotionally dependent on others for a long time, it will be frightening to make independent decisions about our lives and risk the disapproval of others. The only way to begin is by taking small steps that we can handle. Even a baby step puts us farther forward than no step at all. You'll be quite surprised at how much strength, confidence, and pride you get from tapping just a little bit of your hidden inner courage.

Put a three-by-five card on your fridge, mirror, or in your wallet that says: **NOBODY SAID IT WOULD BE EASY!** Too often, we hold the underlying assumption that things *should* be easy, that if we face difficult challenges, it means that we're somehow bad, or the world is against us. With that victim attitude, we find it all too easy to crumble and never discover how strong and creative we really can be. Change isn't easy— ever. But, when we avoid the difficulties in our lives, we never conquer fear. When we face challenges and win, or when we overcome a fear, we experience wonderful feelings of accomplishment and mastery.

Get rid of the attitude that things should be easy, which only encourages you to resist difficulties. Shun the ain't-it-awful and woe-is-me attitudes in yourself, and in other people. Negativity is highly contagious, so if at all possible, avoid being around chronically negative people.

Resistance Magnifies Pain

That the yielding conquers the resistant and the soft conquers the hard is a fact know by all persons, yet utilized by none . . .
        -Lao Tzu

Natural-childbirth classes teach mothers-to-be that the pain of childbirth is greater when you resist it and grow tense with fear. They tell you to "breathe into the pain"—not because deep breathing decreases the pain, but because relaxation increases your ability to accept pain.

In my bereavement groups I meet many people who try to resist their pain. I encourage them to lean into it, to relax into the experience of pain, to give themselves permission to feel it and act on it. This frequently amazes them because most of them have been taught the stiff-upper-lip approach to pain.

Resistance magnifies! The more we resist people or circumstances, the more we draw to us exactly what we're trying to resist. Perhaps that's what Jesus meant when he spoke of turning the other cheek. Resistance causes tension. Tension creates tightness, stiffness, inflexibility; and being stiff, tight, and inflexible makes us vulnerable. In a wind storm, the heavy oak tree resists and the willow yields. The willow, which doesn't stand solidly in the path of the wind but rather allows it to whip through its branches, clearly has the better chance of surviving.

Remember this formula:

Resistance→Tension→Inflexibility→Vulnerability

When you feel yourself resisting (tension will be the first sign), become aware of what or whom you're resisting. What circumstances, memories, attitudes, or relationships are threatening you with pain? Are you magnifying the pain by resisting it?

Acknowledge what you discover about your patterns of resistance. Then accept that the source of pain exists and that you're feeling resistant toward it. Finally, choose to let it be and to act appropriately. Resistance is blind reaction, not free choice. Freedom is created by your ability to choose how you will act.

Resistance can also signal the presence of a power struggle: a desire to be right, to prove a point, to be in control. The only way to win a power struggle is to give it up. Resistance to other people's opinions and feelings is just as useless as resistance to our own. Our pain or discomfort is magnified in direct proportion to our resistance. When your husband is cranky and you think he shouldn't be and resist his mood, you'll feel worse and very likely provoke him further by your resistance. You don't have to stick around and bear the brunt of his mood. Only he can change it, so why resist?

Sylvia hated her husband's constant put-downs about her weight and the fact that he rarely told her he loved her. She entered into the spirit of the power struggle, pointing out every small proof that he was wrong and unloving. In her resistant mood, she didn't see any of the loving things he did. They became like two boxers, jabbing the air in their respective corners in anticipation of the next round. Both were in pain.

As she became aware of the destructive path they both were taking, Sylvia gradually stopped resisting. She didn't give up her rights, but she got off her husband's back. She became more flexible and was able to express her real feelings instead of emotionally lashing out in revenge. She stated her wants and needs, but not in an accusing, judging way. When he couldn't give her what she needed, she became creative at filling her own needs. She stopped resisting him and chose instead to make a better life for herself, not out of resentment for him but out of love for herself.

As Sylvia gained independence, she began to feel less like her husband's victim and more able to reach out to him with love. He'd been resisting her demands for love and affection, but as she demanded less, he felt more like giving.

Khalil Gibran writes:

Your pain is the breaking of the shell that
encloses your understanding.

Even as the stone of the fruit must break, that its
heart may stand in the sun, so must you know pain.

And could you keep your heart in wonder at the daily
miracles of your life, your pain would not seem less
wondrous than your joy;

And you would accept the seasons of your heart, even
as you have always accepted the seasons that pass over
your fields.

And you would watch with serenity through the winters
of your grief.

Give Yourself Credit

*Remember, Ginger Rogers did everything Fred Astaire
did, but she did it backward and in high heels.*
                    -Faith Whittlesey

Our lives are like a bank account in which we make
deposits and withdrawals. How often do you credit the
account of your body, feelings, mind, and spirit? We all have
a *life account*, which we frequently deplete or allow others to
withdraw from too freely. In order to have a comfortable
"balance" and not "see red"—experience frustration and
anger—we need to credit liberally and debit sparingly in all
areas of our lives.

Emotional Bank Account

Debits

Unhealed wounds	Perfectionism
Self-condemnation	Isolation
Overwork	Unreasonable expectations
Judgment	Resistance

A negative life-balance, caused by too many debits,
leads to emotional overdrafts such as:

Low self-esteem	Depression
Overweight	Exhaustion
Emotional dependence	Apathy
Unhappiness	Illness

Credits

Setting limits	Healing old wounds
Self-acceptance	Friends
Exercise	Solitude
Listening to yourself	Love

Credits, which create a positive life-balance, lead to emotional surpluses such as:

High self-esteem	Authenticity
Energy	Joy
Self-confidence	Healing
Courage	Fulfilling relationships

Debit and Credit Examples

Debits:	*Credits:*
"How stupid can you be?"	"Everyone makes mistakes; I'll do better next time."
"Yes" (when you mean "no")	"No, I'm sorry. I am not able to do (____)."
Feeling guilty	Apologizing for real slights and mistakes.
"Everything's just fine" (false smile)	Being truthful about your feelings.
"No, I don't need a thing."	"I could use a good hug!"
"I never do as well as who's-it."	"Great! I did that better than before."
You Messages (saying things you'll regret)	I Messages (not gunnysacking)
Overscheduling and rushing	Realistic goals and schedules
No time for yourself	Relaxing: taking time to smell the flowers
Oversitting; lots of TV	Exercise
Concentrating on your failures	Celebrating your successes

You alone are in charge of your emotional bank account. Other people should be allowed to withdraw or credit your account only if and when you give them permission.

Be liberal with your deposits and frugal with your withdrawals. Never write a blank check!

Nourishing From Overflow

An important part of owning our own excellence is nourishing ourselves and others, and doing so in the best way possible: by *giving* love and support rather than bartering it. We need to build up an ample surplus in our life account in order to have an overflow from which we can give freely, without expectations and strings attached. One of the best ways to build up our account is to make sure we are caring for all parts of ourselves.

To help you gauge how well balanced your life account is right now make a calendar like this one:

DAY	1	2	3	4	5	6	7
PHYSICAL							
EMOTIONAL							
MENTAL							
SPIRITUAL							

Review the four quadrants of your being: physical, emotional, mental, and spiritual. Do you have something going for you in each of these areas or have you become imbalanced? Every day make a note of what you've done for yourself in each of the four areas. Make a commitment to yourself to give time and attention to those areas that need more than you are currently giving. As you do, you nourish yourself and have more to give others as well.

Physical Quadrant

Is your body fit and healthy? Do you treat it with appreciative respect? Try to get at least twenty minutes of aerobic exercise four times a week; even more is better—a brisk walk at lunchtime will do more for us in the long run than the quick-energy infusion of a Snickers bar. Really being disciplined about exercise is probably one of hardest things for most of us, but don't let yourself sabotage your good intentions by excuses such as you don't have time or you look lumpy in tights. It is amazing how much difference a fit body makes in how confident and capable we feel. Give your body good food and plenty of replenishing rest. We cannot run (and most of us do, indeed, run) without effective fuel and restorative periods for refueling. You are your body's only maintenance engineer—it counts on you.

Emotional Quadrant

What feeds you emotionally? Probably anything that increases your enthusiasm, your zest for life, and your feelings of loving and being loved. Whether it's regular conversations with mates, friends, and children, a job well done, or heartfelt laughter—your emotions need nourishment. Need a good cry? Well, why not? Want a raise? Ask!

Listen to your inner signals and you will know when you need emotional energy, and then find a positive source to fill your need. If talking to friends fills you emotionally, make sure that you give yourself the gift of that contact. We are all different, and only we know what best fills the emotional quadrant of our life account. So we need to give ourselves permission to build up our emotional reserves and find ways to infuse ourselves with enthusiasm.

Mental Quadrant

Just as the body and emotions need regular exercise and good food, so does the mind crave the kind of nourishment it can get from inspiring, challenging ideas, books, and conversation. Is your brain too idle? Is your day repetitive, predictable, and not mentally stimulating? Do you find yourself exhaustedly "vegging out" in front of the television? My admittedly biased theory is that too much TV destroys brain cells. We need to give up being drugged by the TV, or by dulling habits, and shake the cobwebs out of our gray matter! We can take a class, read a good book, work a crossword puzzle, or learn a sport. Our brains can be a great ally in our battles with dependence; and the brain thrives on exercise.

Spiritual Quadrant

We are all spiritual beings. *Spiritual* in this context doesn't mean the same as *religious*, although our religion can be very spiritual. Faith in the spirit within is every bit as important to us in our search for the courage to be ourselves as are physical health, emotional stability, and mental clarity.

Spirituality brings us peace of mind and is, above all, an ever-expanding feeling of connection to God as we understand Him/Her/It. Feeling connected to a source higher than ourselves gives us the desire to express love and service to others. Joy is an inherent part of true spirituality when it emanates from the very essence of your self. A walk in the woods, beautiful music, or sitting quietly may create a feeling of spiritual balance and harmony within you.

In order for me to stay balanced, I must spend some quiet time every day with my special books and in prayer or meditation. Find out what feeds you spiritually, and make time in your schedule to practice it daily. Our spirituality is like water; we need it to survive.

Balancing Your Quadrants

Much of our lives today are spent in the mental and physical areas, while our emotional and spiritual quadrants wither. Make a commitment to invest energy in all four areas. Slowly, gently make adjustments to your daily routine. Add a little exercise or a few quiet minutes alone listening to healing and inspiring music. Be aware of your resistance to change and don't undermine your success by demanding the impossible. Make small alterations, build on your successes, and celebrate every change; thus you'll build the positive expectation and energy to change your routine. Soon you'll feel like a different person, with a more interesting life.

Each of these four areas needs deliberate, conscious attention if we're to live as balanced, happy people. Be kind to yourself by honoring each of your four quadrants.

Filling up our own life account before we fill others' takes courage because it seems to contradict the old dictums: think of others before you think of yourself, and, live a life of service and sacrifice. We have little to give when our own life accounts are dangerously depleted. When we fill our cups so that the overflow spills out to others, we'll be able to give more freely and willingly. People will sense that we're sharing from a sense of abundance, so they'll be able to receive without guilt or obligation. We're *giving* to them, and not expecting an equal return. We love best from overflow!

CHAPTER 14

Becoming A Loving And Tolerant Friend To Yourself

Flowers are lovely: love is flower-like
Friendship is a sheltering tree.

-Samuel Coleridge

*I*mplicit throughout this book is the belief that it's essential to become a loving and tolerant friend to yourself. Do *you* act as a sheltering tree in your own life? Take a moment to think about how you treat your friends. Do you express the same kindness and consideration toward yourself? Many of us hold a deep-rooted belief that we don't deserve to be loved. "They" deserve friendship, but for some unfathomable reason, we don't. This is a false belief. We are worthy of love. We *do* deserve our own support and friendship.

One reason we find it hard to befriend ourselves is that we can't forgive ourselves for what we see as our sins. When we evaluate our own performance in life, we immediately call forth acts of kindness, courage, or thoughtfulness that we "should" have done but didn't, or the "bad" things we *did* do.

Is that fair?

Forgiveness

The child in woman is her growing tip, alive throughout our life span. . . . One of the labors of adulthood is to befriend in ourselves those handicapped and underdeveloped parts of our nature which we have set aside.
-M.C. Richards

Of course, we do things that require forgiveness. Elisabeth Kubler-Ross, a specialist in the field of death and dying, calls Earth "the hospital planet." We are all here to recover and heal. Each of us carries internal wounds. We all grope for what is right. Forgiveness creates an atmosphere in which we can best heal.

Think frequently of your inner child. Treat her with gentleness, forgiveness, and tolerance. Whenever I fail, do something foolish, or feel a need to be forgiven, I very deliberately think of myself as "Susie." Reverting to my childhood name helps me remember my inner little girl, and soften my attitude toward myself.

I once received a very helpful button from a minister. It said: **PBPWM GIFWMY,** which decoded means Please Be Patient With Me, God Isn't Finished With Me Yet!

We are always talking to ourselves. In our minds, we create stories about ourselves based on our current experiences as well as on experiences from the past. Too often we cast ourselves in the role of bad girl—that schmucky little kid who never quite measured up, the one who needed to be perfect in order to deserve to live, the victim, the phony, the antagonist.

The people around us when we were young helped us create these stories. Many families have a "bad kid" and a "good kid," a "smart kid" and a "dumb kid," an "everybody's favorite," and a "black sheep," a "responsible kid" and a "baby."

Unconsciously, we carry these labels into adulthood; but now we can rechoose and re-create our stories. We can begin to tell stories about ourselves that are positive, encouraging, tolerant, forgiving, gentle, hopeful, and loving.

Compare:

Good grief, you forgot to mail that report (get a sitter,

whatever)! Can't you remember anything? You're probably getting senile! You have been really stupid lately. You are either sick, or you're really losing it! You should at least be able to remember (___)!

With:

Susie, you are really forgetful lately. What's going on? Are you running on overload, feeling sick, or burning out? Maybe it's time to do something special for yourself.

The first story is very destructive. It lays the groundwork for fears of illness and failure, and definitely isn't conducive to forgiveness. The second story is constructive and self-loving.

The subconscious is like wet clay: it retains the imprint of whatever we press into it and then faithfully reproduces that imprint in our lives. For instance, if we tell ourselves stories that imply we don't deserve to be loved, to succeed, or to lose weight, our subconscious will keep us unloved, failing, and chubby.

Tell yourself optimistic, realistic, and friendly stories. Avoid tragedies and grandiose fairy tales in which you play the goblin or the helpless victim. Sure, you may have warts (So do I! We all do!), but that makes you a candidate for healing, not a frog or a witch!

Support Systems: Everyone Needs Comfort

Peace between countries must rest on the solid foundation of love between individuals.
                    -Gandhi

No one can heal your painful feelings but you, and it's almost impossible to heal them by yourself. We all need to be heard, to be valued, and to be guided. Often our noses are pressed so tightly against the map that we can't see which road to take. A good friend and confidant can be our best mirror—a clear and objective second pair of eyes in a muddled situation.

Isolation kills. We know from studies of orphaned children and animals that babies wither away if they aren't held and cuddled frequently. The clinical term for this wasting-away syndrome is *failure to thrive*. Even as adults, without support systems we, too, fail to thrive.

Support is not one-sided. If we are to receive support, we must support others. Most of us, however, as women, wives, mothers, nurses, secretaries, and so on have been more supportive than supported.

A word of warning about supporting and being supported: A healthy source of support *cares* about our pain but does not *carry* it for us, or try to *cure* it. Nor can we ever realistically expect to carry or cure another person's pain. It's easy to fall into the trap of passively expecting others to do all the healing work for us or to try erroneously to do all the work for someone else.

Watch for the signs of an unhealthy imbalance in your support relationships: fatigue, and a feeling of being overloaded with other people's troubles; or a tendency to avoid certain people and to feel impatient or angry with them. If you see these reactions in yourself, you may be carrying others' pain as if it were your own—perhaps even feeling total responsibility for saving them—which means that you've neglected to honor your own limits and boundaries.

Conversely, if you feel angry at, or abandoned, rejected, victimized, or deserted by your support system (or part of it), ask yourself if you've been expecting those supporters to carry and cure your pain for you. Every person is responsible for his or her own pain. Feel *with* other people, not *for* them.

Be a care-giver, not a cure-giver.

Expand your support systems. Treat yourself to several sources of comfort and guidance. Finding safe places and safe people with whom you are free to be your real self takes time, but it's well worth the effort.

To be contemplative is to be carefully and gently present to ourselves, not in unconscious self-absorption, but in quiet and loving observation.
-Marv Hiles

Observe yourself honestly and gently. You're not "finished" yet, and chances are you won't be finished within this one, short life span. Enjoy the process of re-creating and continually creating yourself. With humor, tolerance, and forgiveness, allow yourself to be transparent to safe and accepting support systems that care for you, and for which you care. Honor yourself and your becomingness. The courage to be yourself is a quest, more easily accomplished in a climate of tolerance, acceptance, and flexibility.

CHAPTER 15

Being Yourself: Honoring Your Past, Your Present, And Your Potential

*Few of us live beyond our three score
and ten years, and yet in that brief time
most of us create and live a
unique biography and weave ourselves
into the fabric of human history.*

-Elisabeth Kubler-Ross

*N*either our past nor our present can describe our potential. Our potential is limitless: we use only a tiny fraction of our resources; the rest atrophies from fear, lack of self-acceptance, and the inability to dream.

To tap our vast potential for freedom and uniqueness, we must begin by honoring our past. Our past, whether it was securely nurturing or devastatingly horrible, gives us the building blocks with which we design our lives. If those building blocks are faulty, it is our task to transform them from impeding our way to building a free and satisfactory present.

The only moment of life we really have is the present—this minute, this hour, this day. All our opportunities beckon us from the center of this moment. *Today* we can improve on our choices, stand up for our rights, and befriend ourselves.

As we work to become truly ourselves, each new day is an opportunity to unfold in the perfect right way.

The Past:	Building blocks
The Present:	Opportunity
The Future:	Potential

A wise and wonderful woman once told me, "The future

depends on a healed past and a well-lived present." Honor your present by living this day in a manner that will enable you to look back tomorrow with pride. Choose well today, and each day learn from whatever sources inspire you to love yourself just as you are—unfinished and still learning. Learn to live with your mate, family, co-workers, and friends as kind and considerate equals.

You have the right, the privilege, and the responsibility to be yourself today.

As you find the courage to be yourself and honor your integrity, your potential will be realized naturally. You'll develop an internal balance and harmony that will enable you to face any circumstance. You'll free yourself from limiting fears and you'll be able to love and serve yourself and others from the overflow of your own abundance.

Our lives and feelings have a natural ebb and flow—a rhythm, which we are often tempted to resist. But we can no more successfully oppose this rhythm than we could stop the ocean's ebb and flow. Far better to let the ocean ebb and, at low tide, take the opportunity to find wonders in the tide pools.

When we can allow our unique ebb and flow—our nights and days, the seasons of our souls—and find the courage to explore and heal our feelings at all levels of their tides, we will find treasures beyond belief; we will discover the courage to be ourselves.

Be gentle with yourself. Growing beyond emotional dependence happens gradually, step by step. Becoming yourself—being free—is a life-long process.

> *Mother God, help me to be Loving*
> *Father God, help me to be Useful*
> *Mother/Father God, help me to be Me;*
> *a unique and valuable expression of You.*

Suggested Readings

The following list is a compilation of titles that either I, my clients, or friends have found meaningful in our quest for the courage to be ourselves.

Bartholomew. *I Come as a Brother*. High Mesa Press, 1982.

Lynn Z. Bloom, Karen Coburn, Joan Pearlman. *The New Assertive Woman*. Delacorte Press, 1975.

Nathaniel Branden. *The Psychology of Romantic Love*. Bantam Books, 1980.

_____. *The Psychology of Self Esteem*. Nashville Pub. Corp, 1969.

Doug Boyd. *Rolling Thunder*. Delta, 1974.

Paula Caplan. *Don't Blame Mother: Healing the Mother-Daughter Relationship*. Harper and Row, 1989.

Dr. Pauline Rose Clance. *The Imposter Phenomenon*. Bantam Books, 1985.

Irene Claremont de Castillejo. *Knowing Women*. Harper and Row, 1973.

Sally Conway. *You and Your Husband's Mid-Life Crisis*. David C. Cook Publishing Co., 1980.

Ram Dass and Paul Gormon. *How Can I Help?* Alfred A. Knopf, 1985.

Colette Dowling. *The Cinderella Complex: Women's Hidden Fear of Independence*. Pocket Books, 1981.

Riane Eisler. *The Chalice and The Blade*. Harper and Row, 1987.

Marilyn Ferguson. *The Aquarian Conspiracy*. Jeremy P. Tarcher, 1980.

Marilyn French. *The Woman's Room*. Jove Publications, 1977.

Nancy Friday. *My Mother/ my self*. Delecorte Press, 1977.

Sonya Friedman. *Smart Cookies Don't Crumble*. G.P. Putnam's Sons, 1985.

Elizabeth Gawain. *The Dolphin's Gift*. Whatever Publishing, 1981.

Kahlil Gibran. *The Prophet*. Alfred A. Knopf, Inc., 1923.

Carol Gilligan. *In a Different Voice*. Harvard University Press, 1982.

Herb Goldberg. *The New Male*. Signet Book, 1979.

Lindsey Hall and Leigh Cohen. *Self Esteem: Tools for Recovery*. Gurze Books, 1991.

Louise Hart, Ph.D. *The Winning Family: Increasing Self-Esteem in Your Children and Yourself*. Lifeskills Press, 1990.

Louise Hay. *You Can Heal Your Life*. Hay House, 1988.

Jean Houston. *The Search for the Beloved*. Jeremy P. Tarcher, 1987.

Laura Archera Huxley. *You Are Not the Target*. Wilshire Book Co, 1963.

Gerald G. Jampolsky. *Love is Letting Go of Fear*. Celestial Arts, 1979.

Karen Johnson. *Trusting Ourselves: The Sourcebook on Psychology for Women*. Atlantic Monthly Press, 1990.

Robert A. Johnson. *She*. Harper and Row, 1976.

_____. *He*. Harper and Row, 1974.

C.G. Jung. *Memories, Dreams Reflections.* Vintage Books, 1961.

David Keirsey and Marilyn Bates. *Please Understand Me: Character and Temperment Types.* Gnosology Books, Ltd. 1984.

Alexander Key. *The Strange White Doves.* The Westminster Press, 1972.

Serge King. *Mastering Your Hidden Self.* The Theosophical Publishing House, 1985.

Elisabeth Kubler-Ross. *On Death and Dying.* Macmillan, 1969.

Mary La Croix. *The Remnant.* Avon, 1981.

Linda Schierse Leonard. *The Wounded Woman: Healing the Father- Daughter Relationship.* Shambhala, 1983.

Harriet Goldhor Lerner, Ph.D. *The Dance of Anger: A Woman's Guide to Changing the Patterns of Intimate Relationships.* Harper & Row, 1985.

_____. *The Dance of Intimacy: A Woman's Guide to Courageous Acts of Change in Key Relationships.* Harper & Row, 1989.

Eda LeShan. *On Living Your Life.* Harper and Row, 1982.

Stephen Levine. *Who Dies?* Anchor Books, 1982.

Anne Morrow Lindberg. *Gift From the Sea.* Pantheon, 1955.

Matthew McKay, Ph.D. and Patrick Fanning. *Prisoners of Belief: Exposing & Changing Beliefs that Control Your Life.* New Harbinger, 1991.

_____. *Self-Esteem.* New Harbinger, 1987.

Alice Miller. *The Drama of the Gifted Child.* Basic Books, 1981.

Raymond A. Moody, MD. *Life After Life.* Stackpole Books, 1976.

____. *Reflections on Life After Life.* Bantam Books, 1977.

Pierre Mornell, MD. *Passive Men, Wild Women.* Ballantine Books, 1971.

John G. Neihardt. *Black Elk Speaks.* University of Nebraska Press, 1961.

Stanlee Phelps and Nancy Austin. *The Assertive Woman.* Impact Publishing, 1975.

Gabriele Lusser Rico. *Writing the Natural Way.* J.P. Tarcher, Inc, 1983.

Samuel H. Sandweiss. *Sai Baba: The Holy Man and The Psychiatrist.* Birth Day Publishing Co., 1975.

Virginia Satir. *Peoplemaking.* Science and Behavior, 1972.

Joy Snell. *The Ministry of Angels.* The Citadel Press, 1962.

Edith R. Stauffer. *Unconditional Love and Forgiveness.* Triangle Publishers, 1987.

Gloria Steinem. *Outrageous Acts and Everyday Rebellions.* New American Library, 1983.

Jess Stern. *The Sleeping Prophet.* Doubleday and Co, Inc., 1967.

Thomas Sugrue. *There is a River: The Story of Edgar Cayce.* Laurel, 1942.

Judy Tatelbaum. *The Courage to Grieve.* Harper and Row, 1980.

Sue Patton Thoele. *The Woman's Book of Courage : Meditations for Empowerment and Peace of Mind.* Conari Press, 1991.

White Eagle. *The Quiet Mind.* The White Eagle Publishing Trust, 1972.

Virginia Woolf. *A Room of One's Own.* Harcourt Brace Jovanovich, 1957.

Paramahansa Yogananda. *Autobiography of a Yogi.* Self Realization Fellowship, 1972.

Personal Note

I hope that reading *The Courage to Be Yourself* has helped you honor, love, and appreciate yourself more and given you helpful guidelines for expressing who *you* truly are. Being the best and most authentic *self* we can be is a precious gift we give ourselves and the world in which we live.

If you would like to share ideas and experiences with me, or if you would like autographed copies of either *The Courage To Be Yourself* or *The Woman's Book Of Courage*, I would love to hear from you.

Sue Patton Thoele
P.O. Box 1519
Boulder, CO 80306-1519